Love From Heaven

Lorna Byrne

Love From Heaven

CORONET

First published in Great Britain in 2014 by Coronet
An imprint of Hodder & Stoughton
An Hachette UK company

1

A CIP catalogue record for this title is available from the British Library

ISBN 978 1 444 78632 3

Typeset in Sabon MT by Palimpsest Book Production Limited,
Falkirk, Stirlingshire

Printed and bound in Great Britain by Clays Ltd, St Ives plc

Hodder & Stoughton policy is to use papers that are natural, renewable
and recyclable products and made from wood grown in sustainable forests.
The logging and manufacturing processes are expected to conform to the
environmental regulations of the country of origin.

Hodder & Stoughton Ltd
338 Euston Road
London NW1 3BH

www.hodder.co.uk

In some cases names of people and places have been changed
to protect privacy.

FOR ALL OF YOU
WITH LOVE

Contents

CHAPTER ONE

We are all pure love

WE ARE ALL PURE LOVE. BUT MOST OF US have locked away this love within ourselves and don't let it out. This love remains there, though. We can lock love away but we cannot destroy it, and we always have the potential to release it. We release it first by learning to love ourselves again. If we are unable to love ourselves, we are unable to love another.

Love is the most powerful force in the world; it comes from our soul, it comes from heaven.

It's love that brings all the joy and happiness into our lives; it's love that helps to steer us in the right direction and drives us forward, regardless of what is going on in our lives; it's love that makes living worthwhile.

Love is like the sun; it's our life force, it transcends everything. And yet the angels keep showing me how little love most people feel for themselves and, as a result, how little love there really is in our lives – and how much more there could be. The state of our world today is evidence of this absence of love.

People often think that love should be all sweetness and light – but the truth is, love frequently hurts. When we open ourselves to love, we also open ourselves up to being hurt. So many of us have learnt from the time we are children to harden ourselves, to lock away our love for fear of being hurt. In locking away this love we make ourselves and our world much more cold-hearted, selfish and sadder. In locking love away deep within us, we diminish our humanity.

Ever since I was a young child, the angels

have been teaching me about love and helping me to see the force of love physically.

I see angels all the time. I cannot remember any time when I have not seen them. From the very moment I opened my eyes after I was born they were there – even though I did not know they were angels. I see them physically as clearly as I see my daughter sitting across the dinner table from me. There has never been a day when I haven't seen angels. Angels are my best friends, my companions and my teachers.

The first time that I was conscious of the angels teaching me about love was when I was about five years old. I was sitting at the kitchen table at home in Old Kilmainham, Dublin, with my mum and da, and my sisters. There was a visitor there, and this person had brought a wonderful treat: a chocolate cake. We children were so excited, as my parents could rarely afford to buy a cake. The table was surrounded by angels. One of the angels told me to watch my father carefully. I did as I was told. As I looked, I started to notice what appeared to be a soft mist coming gently from my father. It seemed to come from every pore of his being, from his whole body, and moved in the direction of my mother. I looked over at Mum and realised that there was a similar mist coming from her. The two mists touched and intertwined. The mist had no colour, but sparkled in the way ice would in the sunshine.

This was the first time I was aware of physically seeing the force of love, and I wouldn't have seen it without the angels' help.

My da was cutting the cake and started to serve me first but my mum stopped him, saying sharply that my sister should get the first slice. My da looked up as if stung and the mist seemed to pull back towards him. The love force I had seen between them had disappeared. The angels told me that my mum's angry comment had made him pull back his love and lock it away. Da was hurt and confused because he hadn't consciously chosen one child over another; he was serving me because I was nearer to him than my sister.

This was to be the first of many times I would

see this love force. I see it when someone is thinking loving thoughts about someone or something. I don't see it with everyone or all the time. To be honest, I don't see it in the abundance I would like. I probably see it with one out of every twenty people that I come across on a normal day.

I am still struggling to describe further what this love force looks like. It's not a bit like an aura or energy, or a ray of light. It's sometimes completely different, yet quite visible to me.

The angels haven't just taught me to see the force of love, they have also taught me to see and measure its intensity – like different temperatures.

 Love is the most powerful force in the world.

Angels have taught me everything I know. Angel Michael and Angel Hosus are probably the angels who have taught me the most – apart from my guardian angel who I am not allowed to talk about. I first met Angel Michael when

I was a very young child. He almost always gives me the appearance of a handsome man. I first met Angel Hosus around the time that I first saw the physical force of love. He gives the appearance of an old-fashioned schoolteacher with a gown and a funny-shaped hat. He is full of knowledge and wisdom and is great at cheering me up and giving me confidence. He started all those years ago in school when I struggled because of my dyslexia and felt very stupid, and he helps me now when I'm writing and doing interviews.

There is another angel whose name I don't know and who I have never even seen properly who is around me when I am being taught about love. This angel was there in the kitchen when I saw the love between my mother and father, and is here with me now as I write about the love force. The angel always seems to be to my right, slightly behind me and out of my line of vision; it's as if I am not allowed to see any more of it. I have no idea why. I have asked about this angel but been told no more about it. I think of it as a special type of teacher-angel sent to help me understand more about love so that I can share it with you.

After the angel with no name had shown me how to physically see the force of love, it started teaching me to measure its intensity. As I was only six or seven at the time, this angel taught me using my fingers. When it wanted to indicate that what I was seeing was love force of an intensity of three, it would bend down two fingers on my hand, to leave three fingers up. It stood behind me doing this, and whenever I tried to turn around to look at the angel I seemed to be physically incapable of doing so, as if some force was stopping me.

If I had learnt to measure love force as an adult, I think the angel might have taught me differently. But this is the way I learnt it, so this is how I still measure intensity of love today.

Most love that I see I measure as being between 1 and 10, but occasionally I am privileged to be shown love that is completely off this scale; I think of it as 100. This number – 100 – was the biggest number I could comprehend as a child when the angel with no name was teaching me about this.

An intensity of love of 100 is so beautiful to see. It reflects the purity of the love coming from the person. It's so hard to describe, though; it's crystal clear and full of a warm light and the force of love shines all around the person and out from them.

It gives me enormous joy when I see love of this intensity. It overwhelms me emotionally and leaves me hardly able to speak. It touches me deeply and stirs the love up within myself. I can feel the effects of it weeks later.

I have no way of knowing whether I feel the force of love differently to others. The angels have told me that everyone has the potential to feel love. It may be, though, that because the angels have made me very conscious of love, and have taught me how to see it physically, that I am more sensitive to feeling it than others.

The angels have also told me that God has allowed me to see the force of love so that I can help to stir up the love that is within all of us.

We are all born pure love. As a baby in our mother's womb, we all love unconditionally. Every one of us, regardless of whether we are wanted, or whether our mums have an easy pregnancy or labour, glow with pure love when we are born. As newborn babies, we know we are perfect and deserving of love and feel pure love for ourselves and everyone around us.

Almost immediately, though, this love force begins to diminish. Even with the most loving mother and father, the baby starts to feel the coldness and lack of love in our world and starts to protect itself by locking away this love inside itself.

The angel with no name taught me to see what it looks like physically when we lock away our love. I was about eight when I was taught this. We were living in our cousin's house in Ballymun after the roof of the house in Old Kilmainham had collapsed. It was a beautiful spring day and I was walking back alone from the shops, having bought some milk for my mother. The angel with no name appeared beside me. There was a group of young boys playing on the street and the angel pointed out a scrawny boy of about five in shorts with a shirt hanging out and told me to look at him carefully. As I did, the boy turned to look in my direction. The angel allowed me to see what looked like a band around the boy's body at heart level. It's hard to describe; it was transparent, like an ice sheet, but hard and cold.

It was as if the love inside him was locked away so that he was not open to being hurt again. The angel asked me if I could I feel anything. I could feel the boy's hurt and pain, and I could also feel the love that wasn't being allowed out. It tore me apart.

I wanted to give him a hug; I walked towards him and, as I got closer, I could see tears in his eyes. I said 'hello' and reached out to him, but as I did he turned away.

The angel told me that he had locked away his love and was afraid of my affection, or anyone else's. I was sorry I had no sweets in my pocket that I could give him. I asked the angel, in the way an eight-year-old would, whether a sweet would help. I couldn't see the angel's face – I have never seen it – but I felt as if it was smiling as it replied that kindness, a loving gesture, from a stranger, or from anyone, could help him to unlock some of this love.

Sometimes unconsciously we unlock some of our love. When we hear of a tragedy in another part of the world we may be engulfed by a feeling of enormous sadness and compassion. We don't know the people affected, but we feel for them. We are touched. The love within us is stirred up and we allow some of it out.

I remember coming across a woman on the street just after the news broke of the 2004 tsunami in South East Asia. I hadn't yet heard about the disaster so I was astonished by the strength of the love I was seeing coming from her, and I didn't know what had caused it. It was like a whirlwind of love coming from every part of her being. It was as if the defences that she had built around herself to protect her from the pain of love had been blown away by the strength of the emotions and love she was feeling.

We feel love through our emotions. And emotions stir us up, helping us to release the love inside us that we may be trying to keep in check. Many of us do our best to stop love from being stirred up inside us, to stop ourselves from feeling this compassion. We decide that if an event doesn't affect us personally, we shouldn't be moved by it – that it doesn't affect our lives. But it does. When we don't let ourselves feel emotions such as compassion and love for our fellow human beings, even strangers, we become less human and this allows emotions such as hate and anger to flourish. We become colder individuals, even to those who we do care for.

We also forget to care for and love ourselves. The angels tell me that loving ourselves is very important for our happiness. I am shown that most people don't love themselves enough. It's as if we have forgotten the importance of loving ourselves.

Again, the angel with no name who has taught

me so much about love taught me how to recognise the force of love when it is directed towards loving one's self. To be honest, I didn't often see it in my own immediate family while growing up. The first time I remember seeing it was when I was seven or eight. I remember going to a Christmas party in my granny's house. There were lots of people there. The angel with no name told me to look into the sitting room. My Uncle Peter was sitting there perched on the arm of a big comfortable chair. As I watched I could see the force of love emerging from him, coming forward, and then moving back towards him like a wave. I could see it was the love force, the same as I had seen between my mum and my da, but it was as if he was being showered with the love that was coming from within. He looked so happy in himself; happy just to be.

His love for himself was so attractive; I wanted to be with him. At that moment he saw me and called me over. I sat happily on his knee and I could feel the comfort and consolation of his own love for himself as well as seeing it. Every so often it would make me giggle, and Uncle Peter would look at me inquisitively as if wondering what this funny little child was thinking.

Love, for ourselves or another, helps us to connect more deeply with our own spirituality, with our soul. If the only thing you take out of this book is to learn to love yourself more, it will make a big difference to your life, and the lives of people around you. In the next chapter I'm going to tell you a lot more about why this is so important, and how you can love yourself more.

Each and every one of us human beings, regardless of religion or beliefs, has a soul. God loves us all so much that he has given each of us a little speck of himself. This speck of the light of God is our soul. We connect more deeply with our soul when we open ourselves up to love.

Love is love; it's always the same, but the angel with no name has shown me that many people have a very narrow view of love – they simply see it as something between a couple, or within a family. I meet so many people who are crying out for love, but they think that the only way to get this love is through a romance, and because of this they are failing to see the love that is already in their lives. They fail to recognise that there are many different ways in which we can love.

One day, when I was about eleven, I was out in the old coach houses at the back of the big hostel where my granny worked in County Clare. The angel with no name came and told me to follow my granddad quietly so I wouldn't be seen. My granddad was a quiet man who had lost a leg in the fight for Irish Independence and, as a result, had difficulty walking. I followed quietly as he walked into one of the sheds and peeked inside. I could see love pouring from my grandfather, even as I saw a look of shock and distress on his face. At the same time I was wondering what was going on.

I watched as he took a white handkerchief

out of his pocket and, with great difficulty, leaned down towards the ground.

When I saw what he had picked up I understood what had happened. In the handkerchief were two tiny birds – baby swallows. There was a swallows' nest high up on the wall and somehow, I have no idea how, these two little birds had fallen out.

To see the look of love on my grandfather's face, and the force of love pouring from him towards them, moved me so much. The angel with no name beside me said, 'This is love. He has locked away so much love because of how hard his life has been.' I thought with sadness of his two children who had, I had been told, died tragically and young. 'This love he feels for these birds is the same as the love you saw your parents show each other. The sadness is that your grandfather finds it easier to show love to a bird than to his family.'

My grandfather moved towards the shed door with difficulty, holding his stick in one hand and the two little birds carefully cradled in the other.

When I walked into the kitchen shortly after this, I found my grandfather had lovingly put the little birds in a box to keep them safe and was feeding them warm milk through a little dropper. He cared for the birds in this way for some weeks, sometimes allowing me to help to feed them, before the birds were strong enough to look after themselves and he let them go free.

The angel with no name has told me that love is love, but that we can love in so many different ways. We all have pure love inside us. We were full of love as a newborn baby and, no matter what has happened to us since then, it is still there. Regardless of what life has thrown at us or what we have done to others, the love within us does not diminish. But we all lock much, or all, of this love away deep within us. We need to learn again how to let it out.

Feeling love for anything helps us to stir up that love within us, and allows us to release more of it. Love is stirred up through personal experience of love: feeling it, thinking loving thoughts, or seeing it. We learn to love from each other.

The angels have told me that we can all learn to love more frequently, and with a greater intensity. This is why I have written this book.

CHAPTER TWO

Learning to love
yourself again

EVERY NEWBORN BABY I SEE GLOWS WITH
love, a glow I see coming from the soul. In a
newborn baby who has just come from heaven
I see the soul much more forward in the body,
and the soul and body seem to be closer
together. This makes the soul of a baby appear
brighter and luminous.

God has created a connection between the soul
and love as a way of enhancing our humanity.

But if we don't love ourselves, all our love for others is diluted. This is why Jesus Christ said, 'Love your neighbour as yourself'. If we don't love ourselves, we are unable to love others.

All babies are pure love. They feel complete love for themselves and know they are perfect, lovable and unique. Yet from the first months of a baby's life I see this glow of love fade, and by the age of ten – and sometimes much younger than this – the glow has diminished greatly as children have locked away a significant proportion of the love in order to protect themselves, in order to stop themselves from being hurt.

God does not allow us to destroy, lose or diminish love. But we can lock much of it away, as if we have put it in a cage and thrown away the key.

If we all glowed with pure love as we did when we were newborn babies, we would live in a completely different world. We would all feel self-confident and know our own gifts. Loving yourself isn't vain, being selfish, or thinking of yourself as more special than anyone else. Self-love is about valuing and loving who you are. No one is perfect – not me, not you – but if we loved ourselves, we would focus on what we enjoy and are good at and we wouldn't worry about the things we weren't good at or felt inadequate about. We would be much less critical of ourselves and others, less likely to run people down. There would be much less jealousy, selfishness or greed. Our lives would be simpler and more joyful.

We would in truth be fully ourselves, the people we have the potential to be at birth, the people God wants us to be. We could make our life on earth like a glimpse of heaven. You might think this is an impossible dream, but God has shown me the evidence that it is a real possibility.

Since I was a child I have been allowed to see what I call 'glowing babies'. These are children who have not locked their love away, but have retained that pure love they had as babies. I probably should call them 'glowing children', or 'glowing young people', but I always associate them with babies because when I see the soul of a 'glowing baby' it shines with that particular luminosity of a newborn.

I can see 'glowing babies' shining so brightly that I wonder that other people can't see it too – but apparently they can't. People are incredibly attracted to them though, without knowing why, and want to be near the 'glowing babies' all the time. 'Glowing babies' are more spiritually evolved; I see their souls and bodies intertwined, and they are a sign of what we all have the potential to be.

Unfortunately, as this world is not yet ready for people like this, they have not been allowed by God to live very long. All the 'glowing babies' I have seen – about a dozen in my life so far – have been born with physical imperfections. The oldest I have ever seen was about sixteen years old; that was a few years ago, and I know she has gone back to heaven now. While 'glowing babies' are here on earth, though, they don't notice their imperfections – they are pure love and, no matter what happens to them, they never lock their love away. 'Glowing babies' are a symbol of hope for the future; they show us what we would be like if we didn't lock our love away.

Sometimes it can be the simplest of things that make young children lose that glow and lock away their love. I have watched it happen on several occasions. I remember bringing my eldest son Christopher to a neighbour's birthday party when he was seven or eight years old. We arrived late and the party was in full swing. The place was packed with excited children, and with angels. I and other mothers drank cups of tea as we chatted and watched the children. The birthday boy's mother was organising party games and there was a basket of inexpensive prizes for the winners. One of the little boys was very excited when he won a prize. The angels in the room surrounded him; he was glowing with love as he reached into the bucket of prizes and excitedly unwrapped the prize he had won, but the prize he had chosen was broken, and he was so disappointed. I saw the boy sigh and he seemed to draw the love back into himself. The angels allowed me to see what looked like a silver band appear around the boy's body at heart level; it was transparent, like an ice sheet, but hard and cold. An angel reached forward and touched the band. I know it was trying to stop the boy from locking away too much love. I watched the glow of love from the boy fade. I felt so sad to see this; my heart went out to him and I said a prayer for him.

I went over to my son Christopher and asked him if he would share the prize he had won with the little boy. Christopher said he would, and we both went over to talk with the other boy. It was too late, though; the boy had drawn in a significant proportion of his own self-love. It was as if he had put it into a cage and had turned a key in order to avoid the possibility of being disappointed or hurt again.

It is so sad. It can be the simplest things; it's not necessarily about major deprivation.

All parents wish to protect their children from life's hard knocks. We can't, though; children are here to live and experience their own lives, the ups and the downs.

As a child, my son Owen had a puppy he adored, and he lavished a huge amount of love on it. Then one day, when he was about seven, the dog got knocked down by a car and was killed. I always remember the sight of him walking sadly through the gate beside his dad, pulling his handmade trolley with the body of his dog on it.

The glow of love that I had always seen shining from Owen was gone; he had locked it away, to protect himself from being hurt again.

By the age of ten most people – and I mean more than nine out of ten – have locked away a significant proportion of their love from themselves and others.

This love never disappears, though; Love can never be destroyed or diminished. It is there locked away inside of you and you have the choice to release it. You can choose to allow yourself to feel it. Doing so will help you to stop destroying yourself and others. It will make your life happier and more fulfilled.

If you can love yourself more, you will be able to love others more and you will be more truly yourself.

The angel with no name has been here with me while I have been working on this chapter and I have asked it how I can help you to learn to love yourself again.

The first thing this angel has asked me to tell you to do is to become aware of how much love you have within you and how you control the key to letting more of this out. Many people have never really thought about the issue of love, and yet it is so important. I am hoping that what I have told you so far in this book has increased your awareness of love and why your life would be better if you could release more.

Many people are shocked when I say that I am told by the angel with no name that nine out of ten people have three-quarters of their love locked away. I was asked whether there was a difference between nationalities or ages, but the truth is I haven't been shown a difference.

It's quite something to think that the vast

majority of people only allow out a quarter of their love. If everyone chose to show even a little more love, it would have a noticeable effect on our world.

 If you can love yourself more, you will be able to love others more and you will be more truly yourself.

Your guardian angel can help you to become more aware of the love you have shut away. Your guardian angel loves you unconditionally. It never judges you, and sees you as perfect in every way. Ask it to help you to see yourself the way it sees you. Ask it to keep reminding you particularly when you start to judge or find fault with yourself. So many of us are good at thinking negative thoughts about ourselves, and think few loving thoughts. If anyone has ever told you that you shouldn't love or value yourself, you should discard this thought – throw it away. When we think loving thoughts about ourselves, we release more love that showers us and makes us more happy and confident; when we think negative or critical thoughts, we do exactly the opposite.

The angels have always told me that everyone is physically beautiful, but so many people lock away love because they judge some part of their body as imperfect. They decide they hate their legs, their skin, their hair and, in focusing on this part, they fail to see the beauty in themselves.

The angel with no name tells me that a good way to release love that is blocked because of feelings of physical inadequacy is to start to look at your physical self differently; to allow yourself to see that beauty in every part of you. One way to do this is to stand in front of a mirror and look at yourself, both the parts you like and the parts that you are uncomfortable with. Start to acknowledge and appreciate that each part of you is unique and beautiful. Say thank you for your wonderful body. Ask your guardian angel to help you to practise this, and to put away negative feelings about any part of your body.

I remember a girl who came to see me in Maynooth many years ago. I could see no force of love coming from her. She was very unhappy and didn't love herself at all. She told me that she felt ugly and hated her appearance. Her guardian angel stood beside her and just said to me, 'Tell her what you see, Lorna.'

I did; I told her what beautiful eyes she had, and what a beautiful smile. I told her how pretty she was – and she was.

I knew, though, that she was having great difficulty in believing me. Her guardian angel told me to ask her whether she liked flowers. She told me she loved them, and that daffodils were her favourite. Her guardian angel then told me to tell her that she should look at herself in the same way as she looked at a daffodil. I did as I was told.

About a year later she came to see me and I could instantly see that she had changed. I could see the force of love wafting from her, and turning and coming back, gently showering her with the love that was coming from within. She was much more happy and confident in herself.

She told me that each time she thought of her looks in a negative way she would think of the beauty and perfection of a daffodil. She told me that she had put a picture of a daffodil in the corner of her mirror to help her remember. She was so grateful, saying that she didn't think she would be still be here without me. I told her it wasn't me – it was that she had listened to her guardian angel and had taken the steps she needed to learn to love herself again.

As you become more aware of the importance of loving yourself, you can start to think of events in your past that led you to lock away love. They may have been small or big, but they devastated you and they are hindering you now from loving yourself. The past cannot be changed, but you can change your future by acknowledging these events and choosing to start to release the pain that they caused. The angel with no name tells me there are different ways of acknowledging these events: talk to someone about them, talk aloud to yourself about them, write a letter to yourself (or someone else) about them. In doing so you acknowledge the hurt that made you lock love away to protect yourself.

Everyone is different. Ask your guardian angel for help in knowing what will work best for you to release these blocks. It may be lighting a candle. Some people need strong physical activity and may benefit from digging the potatoes, or a long hard run to release this hurt.

This is a process; you need to release pain and hurt you have accumulated and you may have to return to it several times. You may find yourself remembering things that you haven't thought of in years, things that perhaps seem trivial now, but hurt you a long time ago. The angel with no name assures me that each time you work on it with full intent you release a little more self-love.

Prayer can of course help in releasing love. God created a connection between the soul and love as a way of enhancing our humanity, so prayer is particularly powerful in releasing love. When I see a surge of love in someone I will sometimes see the soul move because of this connection.

I have asked Angel Hosus for a special prayer

to help people who are seeking to learn to love themselves more, and this is the prayer he gave me:

Dear God
Please help me to release that most
    precious gift you have given me of
    love,
That gift of love that comes from
    Heaven and is connected to my soul.
Amen.

There is such a positive circle between prayer and releasing love. When we pray we are asking for ourselves, or for someone else, or we are giving thanks; we are thinking loving thoughts of ourselves and others and, in doing so, we are releasing more love. The more love we release the purer our prayer becomes because we are able to pray with more compassion, and so our prayer becomes more authentic.

Other people can help you unlock love too. The helplessness, vulnerability and perfection of a new baby frequently helps parents and grandparents to learn to love themselves and others again. The bonding with a new baby can help people to release love unconsciously. It might only be a small amount, what I might call a cupful of love, but that could be a huge increase in that person's love for himself or herself.

Recently I watched a seven-year-old boy and his little sister in a playground. The glow of his love for himself was fading and his guardian angel told me he was very protective of his love, very wary, and it wouldn't take a lot for him to lock most of it away. His little sister, who was about three, was glowing with love.

Another child shoved his little sister in the playground, and I watched as he stood for a moment wondering if he would go and help her. Then I saw a release of self-love as his love for his little sister overcame any reluctance. He went and put an arm around her, standing there lovingly and protectively. His little sister had unwittingly caused him to release more of his self-love. It was so wonderful to see.

Sometimes life is tough and our instinct is

to go on the defensive, and close off even more love. I had a telephone call from a man the other night. I'm not sure who had given him my telephone number, but he rang to tell me how much my books had helped him. He told me that he had five children aged from sixteen down to seven and that he had lost a good job three years ago. He also said that he had found it really tough financially, but had decided to take the opportunity of the extra time at home to get to know his children and his wife better. He told me that up until then his job had always been his first priority and he hadn't spent much time with his family. As I was working on this chapter at the time, I was very struck by how this man had chosen to respond. Many people might have chosen to beat themselves up over having lost their job, to have taken it personally or blamed others; in doing this they would have locked away more love, depriving themselves and others. This man had done the opposite.

We all need to be aware when tough things happen to us, that we have a choice of how to respond. Responding with anger and hate may be an automatic response, but it is never the best one. When we respond with hate we shut away more of our own love. Be aware when your first thought is to respond with hate, you do have a choice.

We also have a choice when something happens that affects our community. When an atrocity like 9/11 happens we can choose whether to respond with hate, or respond with compassion and understanding. When we respond with hate, we lock away more of our love. Showing love, compassion and understanding does not of course mean that justice cannot be sought and people held accountable.

When you love your children you want them to love themselves as much as possible, so I know many people – parents, grandparents, teachers and friends – will want to know how they can stop children from losing their glow of love, from locking it away. The angel with no name tells me that the first and most important thing adults can do is to lead by example. The more love that adults show to themselves and others, the less likely they are to do anything that will lead to the child locking away his or her love. This is why the work on re-learning to love yourself is so important; it matters not just to you, but to everyone around you.

We are all responsible for trying to ensure that as little love as possible is locked away within children. Children are our future, and the only way for the world to evolve as I have been shown it should be is for each generation to be more loving and compassionate than the one before. This is only possible if we support the children around us, and protect and encourage them so that they don't need to lock their love away.

I am occasionally privileged to meet someone who has a very high level of love, and it is such a joy for me when I do. I recently met an elderly man who set up and runs a charity that helps people in dire need.

As soon as I saw him I was overwhelmed by the power of the force of love I could see coming from him. It was like a powerful series of waves that touched everyone in the vicinity, and then turned back and showered him as well. As we shook hands his soul came forward, and I was deeply moved and delighted by what I was seeing. The angels had given me no warning of this. His love, for himself and others, was so strong; he had no ego, only love and compassion. As we talked I saw that his compassion was so deep that he didn't even notice barriers that others see, and that he himself didn't put up barriers by condemning or judging. He is a man of faith with a deep belief in God, but he is humble, and has no sense that he or his religion are better than others. He is very hard-working – and I pray that he is given the physical strength to keep up the work he is doing.

The angels that surrounded him told me that this man had 100 per cent love for himself, and so was able to give love to all. This love manifested in all around him and in his work. I believe that he has had a positive effect on everyone who has come into his life and that because of his enormous love for himself and others he is able to make a difference, sometimes a dramatic one, where others have failed or given up hope. I wish there were more people like him in business, charities and politics. If there were, our world would be so different.

I believe that one of the most important tasks I have been given is to stir up love within people, to make you all aware of how we limit our love for ourselves by locking it away. I don't believe it's any coincidence that a month before I was due to write this chapter I met this man that I have just written about. He is a symbol of hope for us all.

Most of us may not be able to reach the level of love that this man has, but I believe that we all have the potential to love ourselves and others significantly more. If we choose to love more, we will have greater happiness and joy in our own lives and be better able to play our unique role in creating a much more loving and peaceful world.

CHAPTER THREE

The ties of brotherly and sisterly love

I AM ONE OF NINE CHILDREN, FIVE BOYS AND FOUR girls. My brother Christopher died just before I was born. I love all my brothers and sisters even though I don't see that much of them. As a young child I felt in many ways outside the family. When there were family events or outings, I wouldn't be included, with a few rare exceptions. I think this is because my parents believed the doctors who said I was

'retarded', and they were afraid I would do something that would embarrass them. When I was excluded, the angels with me would tell me that my family knew no better, and not to take it personally. To the best of my knowledge I never did anything to embarrass them – other than living in my own world. To me the angels were more interesting than the people around me – including my brothers and sisters – and I did as the angels told me and kept quiet about what I was seeing. So, to be fair to my family, they knew I was different but just couldn't understand me.

The first time the angels taught me about love between siblings was when I was eight or nine. We were living in Ballymun and I loved walking around the different housing estates, accompanied, as always, by angels.

One sunny day Angel Hosus walked with me and when we came to a grassy area he suggested I sit down and enjoy the sunshine. I had been sitting there for a few minutes when I saw three young girls running out from a house across the road on to the green. They were aged from

about ten down to six. They looked alike and were clearly sisters.

They chased one another happily for a few minutes, and then started to play a game that involved clapping and twirling around. It wasn't a game I had seen played before or since – perhaps they invented it themselves – so I have no idea of the game's name, but the girls were clearly having great fun.

There were six angels playing with the girls, in addition to their guardian angels. The angels didn't give a male or female appearance and I could see the wings faintly as if they were an outline drawn with a fine pencil. These angels glowed with a soft pink light that was full of depth but also transparent, difficult as that might be to imagine. They moved gracefully among the children with such looks of care and love on their faces.

Let me explain a little about angels. Angels are neither male nor female, but sometimes they will give me an appearance of being one or the other. I see angels physically as I see people, and I see them all the time. The angels

give me a human appearance to make it easier for me and so as I am able to describe them to you, but being honest it is very hard to describe them as they are incredibly beautiful. I see guardian angels slightly differently to the way I see others. Until I was about five, I saw a guardian angel standing behind everyone, but as guardian angels are extremely bright – much more dazzling than any other angel – I found this very disorienting. So when I was five the angels told me that in future I would be shown guardian angels as a column of bright light behind a person. The guardian angel would only open up and show itself in what I call its full glory if there was some reason for it. I continue to see other angels physically and fully; it is only guardian angels that I am shown more often than not as a column of light.

On this particular day, the angels imitated the little girls, twirling around in the same way, and when one of the girls got dizzy and fell, an angel would fall down with her. Sometimes one of the angels would just fall anyway. In the same way that an angel's feet don't touch

the ground, the angel didn't actually touch the ground when it fell. Sometimes an angel would pretend to be dizzy and have lost its balance and would wind its way through the children as they played like someone who was drunk. The angels were taking particular care of the youngest girl; they would catch her when she fell to the ground, cushioning her landing so that she didn't hurt herself.

I was just sitting there enjoying watching what was going on and had given thanks silently to the girls' guardian angels, who of course were there and never left them, for allowing these angels to take care of these children. Hosus then asked me if I had noticed anything strange – I hadn't. He told me to look again at the youngest girl. Her guardian angel opened up and gave a female appearance. The little girl's guardian angel was dressed in a beautiful flowing gown with all the colours of the rainbow. She was bent over her with her arms wrapped around her. The angel had beautiful golden hands that were clasped in front of her.

I sat there for a few minutes and, just as I

was about to get up, an angel came up on my right side slightly behind me. It was the angel with no name and, as always, I didn't seem to be physically able to turn around to see it properly.

It told me to keep watching the three sisters.

I watched the two older sisters who were having great fun; I could see the force of love flowing between them. I felt the angel touch both my hands and close up three fingers on one of them, leaving seven fingers outstretched. It was telling me that the love between these two sisters was seven.

Then the angel told me to look at the eldest sister and the youngest. I did, and realised that I could see no force of love flowing between them. Watching, I noticed for the first time that the youngest girl was being ignored by the eldest sister, even though she was running after the two of them and doing her best to be part of the fun.

This time the angel touched only one of my hands and bent three of my fingers back leaving only one finger and my thumb still outstretched.

The angel was telling me that two was the intensity of love between the youngest and her oldest sister.

I felt very sad that they loved each other so little and asked why. The angel with no name told me that the oldest sister had not bonded in love properly with the youngest when she was an infant. It also told me that how a newborn baby is embraced and welcomed into its family has a very big impact on the future relations with its brothers and sisters.

Although a newborn baby is pure love it is unable to radiate this love out; it hasn't learnt this yet, just as it hasn't learnt to walk. The love is inside it, but it doesn't know how to give it out. When a mother (or someone else) reaches for the baby with love, the force of love from the mother draws the baby's love out.

Let me tell you what I saw in the Coombe Maternity Hospital when my daughter Ruth saw her new baby sister Megan for the first time. My three older children were already teenagers and were really rather shocked at the idea of having a baby in the family. When Ruth, who was twelve, approached the cot beside my bed rather nervously, I could see a blast of pure love burst from her towards the baby who was several feet away. As this wave of love touched Megan, the love that was inside her came forward and bonded with Ruth's love.

On that day on the green in the sunshine, watching the three sisters, the angel with no name allowed me to understand what had happened when the youngest sister had been a newborn. I could feel her pure love, but could feel no wave of love towards her from her oldest sister. The angel didn't tell me why this had happened, but for whatever reason this baby and her sister had not bonded early in life as is meant to happen and, as a result of this, the level of love between them was now very low.

The youngest girl's guardian angel told me she was keeping trying to form the bond, she was continuing to try and reach out with love to her oldest sister. I have no idea whether she eventually succeeded. The angels tell me that this bond can be formed later in life, but that it requires both siblings to make a conscious choice that they wish to grow in love for each other.

A family came to visit me. There were three children, and the youngest was a six-month-old baby who had been born with a congenital defect and the doctors were saying she wouldn't stay in this world for very long. It was as if the force of love coming from all of them surrounded the family like a cloud. What was most beautiful to see was the constant wave of love coming from the seven-year-old boy and three-year-old girl to their little baby sister. They had been told when the baby was brought home from the maternity hospital that she was very ill and wouldn't be staying long. The love from the older siblings to this little baby in their mother's lap was so strong it was electric.

I saw this little girl and her family several times and each time I was deeply moved by the depth of love between this little baby and her older brother and sister.

The baby died before her first birthday, and

the children grieved deeply for her. But they had been deeply touched by the love they had felt for their little sister and they kept the memories of this love in their hearts. They had learnt how to love deeply, and they would never forget this and it would help them to grow up into adults capable of tremendous love. This shared experience also made the connection between the surviving brother and sister very strong.

I am shown families joined by a thread. Let me try and explain this by describing what I saw last week when my two daughters were home, with my son-in-law and little grandson.

There was a thread that ran through my two daughters and myself, joining us in a circle. My two sons were not there, so the circle didn't extend to them that day. I know, though, that if they had been there physically they would have been included. The thread didn't extend to my son-in-law or grandson. There was another separate thread that was linking Ruth, her husband and child.

I see a thread like this around all immediate

families. We all know that we share blood with our siblings, but I am also shown a deep love connection through this thread. This is a connection that is completely different to the relationship between friends, and that exists throughout our lives, even if we have little contact.

Occasionally the thread to a particular family member looks very thin, almost invisible. This can cause enormous pain to the person excluded and to all the family. Sometimes this occurs because of the love bonding that didn't happen when we were babies, but we also have choices. I remember meeting someone when I was in a packed waiting room in Jervis Street Hospital in Dublin. I was about sixteen, and a young woman of about twenty sat down beside me. She started to talk to me as if she knew me, saying how much she disliked having blood tests and complaining about having to wait so long.

The angel with no name appeared behind me; as always I couldn't see it properly. Two angels appeared beside the young woman. They were dressed in armour of a reddish colour and they stood very still, like soldiers in attendance. I wondered what was happening. The young woman continued to talk to me. She told me that she hated her brother and sister and that she couldn't wait to leave home and get away from them. I was rather shocked by the language she used, but the angel with her told me to ignore her language: that it was the only way she knew how to communicate her frustration.

She continued to go on about her brother and sister, saying she hated even the sight of them. I was taken aback by the depth of her hatred for them. The angel with no name asked me, without words, to put the question to her, 'Do you love them even a little?' I took a deep breath, aware that I might get a torrent of abuse, and posed the question.

She glared at me and snarled, 'Not even the tiniest bit.' She was very angry with them, and now with me as well.

The two angels beside her each put a hand on her shoulders as if to reassure her. At that moment a nurse called her name. She left without saying goodbye or even casting a glance in my direction.

 The connection between brothers and sisters is completely different to that between friends, and it exists throughout our lives, even if we have little contact.

The angel with no name told me that her brother and sister loved her and had never intentionally done anything to hurt her. I was so sad at her lack of love. 'Can it not be changed?' I asked, 'Can she not learn to love?'

The angel with no name replied, 'You know she has the love inside, but she has locked it away. She needs to realise this and choose to release it. By asking that question you have made her conscious of her own lack of love and that is why she got so mad at you. But now she is aware of her lack of love, and she has a choice;

she can choose to try to let love grow between herself and her brother and sister, or she can continue to close her heart. It's her choice.'

In this instance, I was asked by the angel with no name to intervene and help the young woman release some of the love she had locked away. We are often asked by angels to give messages to another person, but I'm talking about something much more than that here. It's as if on these occasions we are asked, unbeknown to our conscious selves, that we allow our love to come forward and touch the love that is locked away in another's heart. It's as if in touching them with our love we turn the key to release the love that is locked away inside that person. This of course doesn't only happen in relation to siblings, but can happen anywhere that love is locked away.

We all have the choice to reach out to our brothers and sisters. No matter what differences we might have had, it's never too late.

Some years ago I was sitting talking with a friend of a friend. This woman, who was in her mid-thirties, cried as she talked about her relationship with her brothers and sisters. Behind her stood her guardian angel, tall and rigid with arms stretched out on either side of her as if to protect her. The guardian angel was dressed in what looked like armour of a bottle-green colour. The armour seemed to be made of long, thin, rigid rectangles of a metal-like material.

The woman told me that she was from a big family, and that she loved her brothers and sisters very much. But they were constantly running her down, criticising her and her husband and their children. She told me that this had been going on for years and that it was tearing her apart. She said she would do anything for them and she constantly reached out to them, but all her advances were rejected; no matter what she tried it just didn't seem to work.

She told me, though, that she wouldn't give up, that she would do all she could to build better relationships with her brothers and sisters, and asked me to pray for a miracle.

Over the years I have thought of her at times and said a prayer for her and her siblings.

I met her recently and I immediately knew something had changed; it wasn't just that she looked much happier, but her guardian angel was now wearing armour that seemed to be soft and flexible rather than rigid and defensive.

People always want to know what their guardian angel looks like. The truth is, though, that the appearance a guardian angel gives me can change, depending on what is going on in the life of the person it is guarding and the message it wants to give. In this case, the guardian angel was showing me that this woman had become softer and lowered her defences.

The woman's mother had died after an illness, and during the year when the family was focused on caring for their mother the coldness between her and her siblings seemed to diminish. They had come to know and appreciate each other more.

The pain and grief of their mother's illness and death had softened them and opened them up to rekindling the love they had for each other.

*   *   *

The sadness and pain surrounding the death of a parent, brother or sister can bring with it an unexpected gift, and help families to become closer. It can help to bring shared memories to light, and be a reminder of love that was shared in the past. Sometimes this happens over the years that follow the death rather than in the immediate period afterwards.

The angels always tell me that when parents die, they want their children to become more loving and united. Strange as it may sound, those who have gone to heaven can do much more for those they loved on earth than they could ever do while here, so parents continue from heaven to work to bring siblings together. This happens in two ways: they can pray more powerfully with God on behalf of their children when they are in heaven; and they can also be present around their children when they are needed, giving messages to siblings and other family members to help resolve disputes and bring the siblings closer.

Of course, not everyone has brothers and sisters. Some people are only children.

Sometimes I will see a stronger thread between the parents and an only child and I know this can help, but the reality is that the parents are likely to go to heaven before the child and leave it without blood family members. I have met many only children who are very good at building strong bonds with friends, thereby creating substitute brothers and sisters.

Many of us with siblings don't appreciate what we have. Often we don't realise quite how much we love them until it is too late, and even if we realise that we love them we often lack the courage or are too embarrassed to say the words 'I love you' to our brothers or sisters.

I was doing a book signing in Scotland a couple of years ago when a man of about forty came and sat beside me. His guardian angel was holding on to him tightly; the angel's wings were a beautiful shade of red and were wrapped around the man. The angel with no name appeared on my right, slightly behind me, as the man's guardian angel asked me to give the man some extra time to talk.

The man reached out and took both my

hands as he told me about his younger brother Paul who had been killed in a car accident. Paul was much younger than him; and when Paul was born, the man had just left home to go to university. He told me that he hardly took any notice of Paul, never spent any time with him or played with him – even though Paul used to ask him to. He said he didn't realise he loved Paul until he was killed, and that now he felt devastated and full of regrets.

The angel with no name gave me a message to give him: 'Paul loves you'. I said, 'He wants me to remind you of all the times he would rush to open the door when you came home and would greet you with a big smile.'

The man looked at me with tears rolling down his face. 'How come I never saw his love for me? How come I didn't know I loved him? I regret deeply that I never told him that I loved him.'

The man was silent for a moment, then continued, 'I really loved him, Lorna, and now it's too late. I can do nothing about it.'

I held his hand tightly and said, 'Yes you can.

Think of Paul and tell him you love him; he will hear you.'

I blessed and prayed over him and asked for his heartache to be eased, but I know the pain will never fully go.

Remember to show your brothers and sisters that you love them and, if you can, take your courage in your hands and tell them to their faces that you love them.

CHAPTER FOUR

Friendship is love

MANY PEOPLE DON'T LIKE TO ACKNOWLEDGE that friendship can be love and there will be some who will ask why there is a chapter on friendship in a book about love.

The angels tell me many people only realise that they loved a friend when it is too late, that much of the time we play down friendships, containing them, and not allowing the love that is in them to grow. The angels also have told me that it would be a huge step if we could only acknowledge to ourselves and to our good friends that we love them; that then our lives would be more fulfilled and happy.

Yesterday, while I was thinking about how to write about friendship in this chapter, I went to Kilkenny, a city near where I live. It was a Sunday and the city was very busy. The angel with no name appeared and brought my attention to a large group of teenagers; there were about eight girls and perhaps three boys. This angel told me that the angels were teaching the group about friendship and love, and were going to use them to help me to understand it better too.

I watched one boy of about sixteen chatting with the girls as he walked along. His guardian angel gave a male appearance and was dressed in red clothing that seemed to be moving all the time. The young man was the tallest of the group, but his guardian angel towered over him. The guardian angel spoke to me silently, saying, 'Lorna, do you notice this young man has no barriers up?'

As the angel said this, he gestured with his hands around the young man's body, as if demonstrating that there were no barriers around him. I looked from the young man to the girls, and I saw something I had never in my life noticed before. It was as if the girls had a barrier in front of them which stretched from head to head, a little like a shield a police officer would hold in a riot. At first I thought it was just one barrier protecting all the girls, but then I realised that that impression was simply because the girls were so close together. Each girl had an individual barrier in front of her which was fine and clear.

The young man was the only one who had no barrier or screen up. His guardian angel told me, 'He is open and willing to allow friendship into his life. He is confident, and happy that these girls are his friends; he is not thinking of romance, he is just happy to be here with them, and feels privileged that they are his friends.'

I asked the angel with no name about the

barriers in front of the young girls. I was told that they thought of themselves as friends, but that they had not taken down the barriers, so it wasn't real friendship. It was conditional friendship. The angel said that they were afraid to show their true selves, they were afraid to take the risk of showing their friends who they really were and what they really thought.

The angel also told me that this particular group of young people was a safe group for them to let down their barriers and learn about friendship. Their guardian angels were encouraging them to move from being little more than acquaintances to becoming real friends. I was told that if they did allow real friendship to grow, they would help each other through their final years of school and their exams and into adult life.

Friendship is a risk, for all of us of all ages, not just for teenagers. Showing our true self is a risk, but it is a risk worth taking. Friendship is so important; it's something we need to grow and develop and it is something we all long for.

The angel with no name asked me to look at two girls who were chatting animatedly to each other a short distance behind the main group. I could see this barrier in front of the two girls, but every so often as they walked along the barrier in front of one of them would disappear. I was fascinated and pleased to see her dropping the barrier. She was tentatively taking the first steps towards becoming a real friend. As the girls walked past, I said a prayer that they and the entire group would learn to drop their barriers and create real friendships.

 If we could acknowledge to ourselves and to our good friends that we love them, our lives would be more fulfilled and happy.

Friendship helps us to grow and become more caring and understanding. I watched this at work with the supervisor of a supermarket where I have shopped over the years. One day some years ago I was doing my shopping and I saw him surrounded by angels. The angels with him told me that he was being driven crazy by a new young man who had come to work in the store. He was able to deal with it, though, because of what friendship had taught him over the years.

The angels told me that over ten years before, when he had started work in the shop, he had considered himself superior to the people who were working for him. He didn't think that work was any place for friendship, and he didn't think any of the people working for him had anything to offer him as a friend. He certainly wasn't a friend to anyone who worked there, and was a rather cold and uncaring supervisor.

One day, though, about six months into the job, he himself made a big mistake on a delivery and was in a state about this. He feared he would lose his job. One of the people who worked for him came and told him not to worry, that he and some of the other colleagues would help to sort the problem out. They did. The angels told me that this was the first time that he had lowered his barriers to allow friendship into his place of work.

His friendships over the years at work had given him an insight into lots of different people. The angels tell me that friendship helps us to see fragments of the world through other people's eyes, and this opens us up to the fact that our perspective may not be the only one, and may in fact be wrong. Friendship makes us more compassionate, more aware of our own imperfections, and this helps us to learn to give other people a chance. This man had learnt a lot and this is what gave him the patience to work with the new young colleague, even if he was irritating him.

I have to acknowledge that my own experience of friendship has been very limited. No matter how much or how often I have reached out to make friends, the angels didn't allow it to happen. Sometimes when I meet someone and they offer friendship the angels would tell me that I could only have this friendship, for a short time, to a certain depth, and then

I would need to let them move on. The angels have never fully explained why I am not allowed to have more friends, so I have no idea why this is.

Of course, I do have the consolation of the constant company of angels and consider Angel Michael, who is in fact Archangel Michael, and Angel Hosus as my best friends. So in this I am blessed.

This lack of friends throughout my life has given me a great understanding of loneliness and compassion towards it. Loneliness is heart-rending, and what is particularly sad is that so much loneliness is unnecessary. People can do so much to take their own loneliness away.

I remember being asked to help one particular woman – I met up with her in Bewley's in Grafton Street in Dublin. She was in her forties. I know she was married but she never mentioned any children, and she told me she was very lonely. Her guardian angel, standing behind her, gave a female appearance, and seemed to be very broad, taking up more space than a guardian angel usually does. The angel was dressed in very feminine robes of mauve and pink. I could see long strands of fine blonde hair – it's quite unusual for me to see an angel's hair in this way. The look on the angel's face was of tremendous compassion. This guardian angel told me I was to tell her to go and join a club. I did.

The woman was horrified at the suggestion. She told me that only people who were pathetic joined clubs! I know she was shy and lacked confidence, but she was also very judgemental about the sort of people she would meet in a club. We talked for some time and, to be honest, I wasn't sure whether she was going to take any of the proactive steps she needed to take to get out of her loneliness.

Out of the blue, a year or so later, I got a short text from her telling me that she had in fact listened. She had joined a gardening club and it was the best thing she had ever done. The text also said that she had made lots of friends and was going on lots of outings. I said a little prayer of thanks that she had listened to her guardian angel.

Too many people look to their families to fill the loneliness, but you need friends too – people who have different interests and different concerns. Friendships open new horizons; they help you to gain confidence and encourage you to do things that you might not normally consider.

I always think it's sad when I meet people who are so preoccupied with finding a romantic partner that they miss out on making friends.

There was a woman who used to come and see me, seeking help, before my husband died. She was a good-looking woman of about thirty and she was obsessed with finding a husband. She had a few female friends, but each time a man came along she ignored them. Time and time again she met men and broke up with them. I would see her off and on over the years and she would complain to me of her loneliness, a loneliness she believed could only be solved by a romantic relationship. Her guardian angel kept telling me she needed to make more friends, female and male, and to stop viewing every man as a potential partner. She never seemed to listen, though, and I got tired of having the same conversation with her and started to avoid seeing her if I could.

One day a few years ago she asked to meet me for coffee. I was free that day so it was possible, but I really didn't want to waste any more energy on her. My guardian angel, though, told me that I should meet her; that I would be surprised. I was intrigued by this, so we met. As soon as I saw her I knew something had changed because of the love coming from her. Finally, she was starting to love herself.

She told me that a year before she had joined a group of volunteers who work with homeless people. They ran various services including a soup kitchen, and a street outreach programme. She was enjoying helping the homeless, but what had made the big difference was the group of people she was working with. She had got to know lots of the volunteers – men and women – and had learnt for the first time in her life to look on men as friends rather than only as potential partners. She was full of life as she chatted about the different men and women she had come to know and regard as friends.

She made no mention at all of her love life. It never came up. Before I left, her guardian angel told me to ask her if she could see herself getting romantically involved with any of the men she had met. 'Lorna, they are my friends!' she said, with a degree of surprise. I was delighted with her reply, as it showed she was no longer seeing men only as potential husbands, but had finally learnt that members of the opposite sex make great friends.

There is of course another form of loneliness: that of people who have loads of friends, but have never let the barriers down and allowed their friends to see the real person. Sometimes I think this is the saddest form of loneliness because such people have chosen to deny themselves the opportunity of real friendship.

I remember years ago when Joe, my husband, and I were going on a rare night out to a charity fundraiser.

At this fundraiser was a good-looking young man in his early twenties, who was going around chatting with everyone, the life and soul of the party. His guardian angel was very tall and powerful-looking, dressed in armour of silver and gold. I knew by his appearance he was trying to give the young man courage and strength. The guardian angel told me that despite all the young man's apparent sociability, he wouldn't let any of his friends close to him. They might open their hearts to him, but he never let anyone see the real person he was. This young man was in fact extremely lonely – but he disguised it brilliantly. Lots of the other young men there considered him a good friend. They may have been his friend, but he didn't know how to trust them back; he felt unable to show any vulnerability and so kept his defences up.

Some fifteen years later I opened the newspaper and there was a small article about a man who had taken his own life. The angels with me told me it was this same young man. I felt so sad knowing that he might not have taken his own life had he listened to his guardian angel and been able to let down his barriers to his friends and admit that he, like all of us, wasn't perfect.

We all have to show our vulnerabilities. We all have to learn that it is OK to be vulnerable and that no one is perfect. Friendships are often the best place to show this vulnerability. The next time you are with your friends, observe who is allowing their true selves to show, warts and all, and who is keeping the barriers up, presenting themselves and their lives as perfect. It may be you.

If it's others who are not trusting, try to give them the support and encouragement to share more openly.

If you notice it is you, consciously try to let your barriers down and trust a little more. You can do it bit by bit, every now and then, until you feel safe.

Of course it's a really big question to decide who it is you should trust. My youngest daughter is still only a teenager. I tell her that when someone new comes into her group of friends she should allow that person to earn her trust; that she should listen to what her guardian angel is saying and, if she has any concerns after that, not to trust the person completely. We all have to learn to listen to those gut feelings that we are given.

It is of course a sad fact of life that sometimes friends betray trust. There was a woman I used to see often when my children were little as I walked to and from the shops most days. She was much the same age as me – late twenties or early thirties. I never knew her name or had a proper conversation with her, but we would smile and greet each other as we passed.

The one thing I always noticed about her was her self-love. The force of love always seemed to waft from her, coming forward and then moving back like a wave towards her, showering her with love. It filled her with confidence and self-belief. She always seemed happy.

One day, as she came towards me, she looked very sad, but what really shocked me was that there was no love coming from her. Instead, it was as if there was a transparent iron band around her heart, like an ice sheet, hard and cold.

I asked Angel Hosus, who was walking with me, what was wrong. All he replied was, 'The only thing you can do, Lorna, is just say hello.' I did this, but the woman didn't even lift her head in response to my greeting.

I then asked Hosus what I could do to help. 'All you can do is smile and say hello to her when you meet and say a prayer for her. Her guardian angel is working very hard with her.' I asked Hosus again what was wrong, but still got no answer.

The woman remained in my prayers in the following months and every fortnight or so I would pass her on the street. Her guardian angel always had its arms wrapped around her lovingly. Sometimes this guardian angel would be holding a bright light in front of her at heart level, trying to help her to see the light that was in her life. I would smile and say hello, but I never got a response from her.

Then suddenly she seemed to disappear, and

for about three months I didn't see her at all. I worried about her, and prayed, but there was nobody I could ask about her as I didn't even know her name. When I asked Hosus about her, he just told me to keep praying.

I will always remember the day I saw her again. I was walking home from the shops, when the angels around me told me to walk home the long way, by Maynooth College. Just as I passed the college I saw this woman in the distance, walking towards me; her guardian angel was still holding on to her, but now he was a little more upright. I was happy to see this. As I got closer to her, Hosus appeared beside me. He told me to slow down as I said hello.

As I got closer to the woman, I gave her a big smile, but she didn't smile back. I said hello and, this time, she said hello. I stopped, using the excuse of fixing the blankets on my little daughter Ruth, who was asleep in the pram.

The woman stopped too. Her guardian angel remained with its arms wrapped around her, whispering to her. To my surprise the woman suddenly started talking. The words seemed to pour out of her in a torrent. She told me her best friend was not talking to her any more. She also said that there was a secret that she and her friend had shared for years, but she had made a terrible mistake and told someone else. The woman didn't tell me what the secret was, only that she had kept it for years but now lots of people knew what it was. Her friend's secret was no longer a secret, and it was her fault.

All her hurt and pain poured out as she told me that she had broken the bond of friendship and that her friend had rejected her. She was completely shattered.

Looking at her, it was as if the love for her friend was bursting forward, but instead of looking like the love force that the angel had shown me between my parents, it was as if this love had been shredded, as if it had been slashed with a sharp knife.

'We have been best friends since we were children, and have always lived near each other and done everything together. She has always been one of the most important people in my life.' She added, 'I really miss her, but no matter how I try to apologise, she will not talk to me. She has told me that to her I am dead. I can't live with this, it's like one-half of me has been ripped apart.'

Her eyes were full of tears, which then rolled down her face. I listened attentively, never saying a word.

She poured her heart out to me. It was as if for that moment I was a substitute for the friend she had lost. Her guardian angel had been encouraging her to unburden herself to me, and she had finally listened. Sometimes friendship is a precious gift just for a few minutes, and that was what was happening here. For a fleeting moment we were friends, even though I didn't even know her name and have never spoken to her since.

Her guardian angel looked up at me for a moment and told me I was to tell her that she was to hold on to the love that she has had for her friend for all of these years, that she was to hold it in her heart, and every time she thinks of her friend to say a prayer and ask for good things for her and her family – to tell her that even if her friend never speaks to her again, she must always cherish that special friendship and how precious it is.

Her guardian angel told me to assure her that she would make new friends. As I did this, the woman seemed to take a deep breath. She then said goodbye and walked on. I didn't see her again for a long time.

The next time I saw her I was walking with my son Owen from the football grounds. She was walking along chatting to another woman and I could see her guardian angel was no longer holding on to her. I could see she still had a band around her heart, but it wasn't tied as tight. She was allowing some of her love out, but I could see nothing like the level of love I used to see before she let her friend down.

The woman didn't say hello, perhaps she didn't see me, but her guardian angel spoke to me without words. He told me that she still had an empty space in her heart in the hope that one day she would be reconciled with her friend.

But she was now reasonably happy and content and had new friends, although she knew they could never take the place of her old best friend.

The angels have told me that deep friendship brings huge responsibility with it. What binds people together in powerful and close friendship is trust, the confidence that you can trust that good friend with everything in your life. When this trust is broken, as it was in this case, the friendship can be shattered, and leave the people involved heartbroken.

Friendship is so precious, and even if it has broken up in difficult circumstances like this, both friends need to hold on to the specialness of what they once had. They may not be able to rekindle the friendship, but they must not forget or dishonour what they had. They still have a responsibility to the friendship, an obligation of trust. They must not speak badly of each other. They must always remember the love they had, and keep it safely in their hearts, even if their hearts are broken, treating it as the precious thing it is.

Thinking loving thoughts about friends,

particularly after a rift, is important. In fact, thinking loving thoughts about anyone and everyone is important. When we think lovingly of someone and wish them well, it's a form of prayer, and is received by God as such. When we think loving thoughts, we release some more of the love that we have locked away.

Sometimes time heals rifts in friendship. The angels have told me that while people are still alive, friendship can be rekindled – even if it is with less intensity. It may be that as time passes, perhaps many years, these woman could meet again in different circumstances and find that over time the one who was wronged has forgiven the other, that friendship, even on a lesser level, can come back into their lives.

Keep the door open so that lost friends can walk back into your life. Friends are too precious to waste. If you and a good friend have fallen out over the years, the angels tell me you should consider reaching out again, particularly if an opportunity arises. Stretch out your hand, but do not take it personally or take offence if your approach is rejected.

We all have the capacity to have more friends than we have at this moment. Life is fast changing and there are times when friends have to move on. Sometimes it's because friends move house, sometimes a friend who we have worked with for many years changes his or her job. The world has become smaller for all of us. Sometimes circumstances mean that friends drift away. This often happens, for example, when a friend becomes a mother and has children who take up all her time and energy.

Whatever happens to us in life we need to keep the door open to new friendships; we need to keep open the possibility that an acquaintance, who you have hardly noticed, has the potential to become a good friend; that a stranger who you have yet to meet could become a very important friend to you.

Friendship can be very hard work at times. It can take a lot of effort. If you are lonely, it takes an effort to overcome shyness and lack of confidence to go and meet people and discover potential friends. Friendship requires you to put yourself out when you don't feel like it, to make the effort to go and meet a friend when you feel like putting your feet up in front of the television. Everything that is worth doing requires effort, and friendship is no different.

I am struggling as to how to end this chapter, but my guardian angel has told me that all I have to do is remind you that friendship is love, and love is what makes our lives worth living.

CHAPTER FIVE

Love of strangers

SISTER MARY HELD UP A TIN BOX WITH A picture of an African child on it. Angel Hosus stood beside her, imitating her every gesture. I tried not to laugh.

'I want you all to give up sweets for Lent and put the money you save into this box for the little children in Africa. We may not have a lot, but these children are poorer than us.'

I was about eight at this time and we did a charity collection for children in Africa each

Lent – the forty days leading up to Easter observed by Catholics. As I listened to what Sister Mary said, something struck me as strange, but I couldn't put my finger on it.

The nun started to give out leaflets about the charity for us to take home to our parents. As she walked past our desks, the light of her guardian angel opened and embraced her lovingly, looking at her with such gentleness. I looked over at Angel Hosus, who was standing in the corner. He knew what was going through my mind. I silently said one word: 'love'.

Watching Sister Mary's guardian angel showing love for her, I realised with shock that she hadn't told us we should give money to these children because of love; she hadn't told us that she loved these children in Africa (even if she didn't know them) and that we should too.

Angel Hosus tried to comfort me, saying, 'Lorna, she just forgot to say "love".' He continued, 'Lorna, do you love those children in Africa?'

'Yes,' I said, 'I love them.'

The nun had now reached me and handed me a leaflet.

'You forgot to say "love"!' I blurted out.

The nun glared at me and said, 'Be quiet, you silly child.'

I was used to being ignored and called names so that didn't unduly worry me, but what did worry me was the idea that maybe Sister Mary knew nothing about love.

Each year after that there was a Lenten collection, and in all the years I never ever heard anyone mention loving these children in Africa, loving these strangers, as a reason for helping them.

Some years ago, while driving with my husband Joe, we came across a car accident. It had just happened and there were no emergency services there yet. There was a woman lying on the ground seriously injured, and kneeling beside her comforting her was a passer-by. This passer-by didn't know the woman – she was a stranger to her – but I was overwhelmed by the love I could see and feel coming from her towards the injured woman. She was leaning over the woman, who was covered in blood and clearly in great pain, stroking her and talking quietly to her, reassuring her that help was on the way. The guardian angel of the woman who was helping opened up. The angel was wearing a cloak that cascaded down over the passer-by and touched the injured woman. It looked very beautiful, but strange. Then I realised that the guardian angel was using this cloak as a funnel to help the passer-by to direct her love to the injured woman on the ground, to make sure that she would feel as much as possible the love that was being poured out on her. It was so beautiful to see and to feel this love.

An ambulance arrived shortly after, and the woman was taken to hospital. I asked the angels whether she would be OK and was assured that she would be.

I am still moved when I think of the tremendous love that flowed from this stranger towards the injured woman. We each have the potential to love strangers because we are all connected; each and every one of us has a soul, and all of our souls are one; they are all a part of God.

We have a huge potential to love strangers, but a lot of the time we make a conscious decision to become cold-hearted and to hold back the love we feel. We are afraid of being overwhelmed; that if we let down our barriers, we will care too much and be called upon to act. Some people fear that there will not be enough love to go around, and that as a result their love will be used up.

There is no shortage of love; there is an abundance of it. The truth is that the more we reach out to strangers with love, the more love we will have in our own lives.

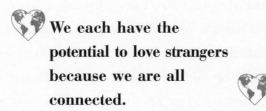 **We each have the potential to love strangers because we are all connected.**

I meet many people who are seeking their soulmate, the person who they believe they are destined to marry and grow old with. The truth is that your soulmate may be a stranger in need who crosses your path very briefly, or a child who is hungry on the other side of the world.

I remember when my son Christopher was in hospital as a child. The angels told me to pay attention as a particular doctor visited the ward. The doctor, a man in his fifties, examined each of the children and talked to them and their families. There was a little boy of about three in the bed by the window. He was clearly very sick and there was no family with him. As the doctor reached the child, the doctor's guardian angel and the child's guardian angel opened up – at exactly the same moment. The little boy reached out his arms to the doctor. I could see the force of love going from the child to the doctor, and being returned with such intensity. I asked the angels a question – and they confirmed what I thought. These two were soulmates. The doctor couldn't work out why he felt so much for this patient, and was heartbroken because he knew he couldn't save him, that the boy was going to die shortly. I know now that it was very important for them to meet, even briefly, and I believe it was partly to help the doctor to learn more about love and compassion.

We each have a soulmate, a soul we knew in heaven and have a special connection with, but in most cases this person is not our romantic partner, and you will not necessarily even meet. Our world would be a much better place if instead of searching for our soulmate as a romantic partner, we considered the idea that a stranger in need could in fact be our soulmate.

As I have been working on this chapter, I have been asked about the difference between becoming cold-hearted and locking away our love. They are in fact very different. We don't usually choose to lock away our love. Most of the time it happens as an involuntary reaction to things that happen around us. Cold-heartedness, on the other hand, is something that we can choose to turn on or off. Unfortunately, I have to say that I am seeing more people these days choosing to be cold-hearted. I keep talking of the hope I see in the world, of the areas where I see things improving, but I believe we are behind where we should be in loving strangers, and I want to make people more conscious of the choices they can make to reject cold-heartedness.

When we choose to become cold-hearted, when we make a conscious decision not to get involved, it doesn't just affect the person or people we decline to help; it affects us and everyone around us.

I am not of course saying that people have to help everyone – that's not possible – but sometimes God and the angels will touch you, or move you, to help a stranger and make you feel compassion for that individual – or even a particular cause. When you feel this compulsion to help, I would ask you to help in whatever way you can, no matter how small it is; it may just be to give a smile.

Sometimes there is nothing we can do to help a stranger but say a prayer. I remember one lunchtime being in a pub in Kilkenny, which served food. I was with my daughter Megan, who was about nine at the time. The television was on and, as the news headlines came on, a shocked hush fell over the pub. A school bus had crashed and several teenage girls had been killed and many more injured. Hearing the news, I know I wasn't alone in feeling like crying. We were all touched with love and compassion for those affected, even though none of us personally knew any of the teenagers involved or their families. I could see a rush of the force of love being released from everyone there in response to this wave of compassion. When we allow ourselves to love strangers and to care what happens to them we release more of the love for ourselves that we have locked away.

We were a long distance from the crash and not in a position to do anything to help on a physical level, but I could see a flow of angels of prayer going like a reverse waterfall to heaven so I know that many of the people there joined me in saying a silent prayer for all those affected.

Slowly people started to talk to one another, to people who they hadn't known five minutes earlier; we had all been touched by this tragedy, and as a result had been transformed into a loving and caring community.

This happens all around the world; sometimes at a local level and sometimes at a global one. We feel our connectedness, our love. We feel that even if we are strangers, we are all part of a wider whole.

CHAPTER SIX

Loving your parents as people in their own right

SO MANY MEN AND WOMEN I MEET DON'T know their parents as people, as individuals with personalities and lives of their own. They never let their relationship move on from being a child–parent relationship to being an adult relationship where you know each other properly.

Recently I found myself in a café in Dublin I had never been to before. I tried to find the

French café that my daughter Megan likes, but the angels wouldn't let me. After some time searching for it, they told me I needed to go to a different café.

As I walked in, the angels with me told me to say hello to one particular man. His head was down and he certainly didn't look interested in being disturbed. I gave out to the angels, saying, 'Well, if I say hello to him, his guardian angel will have to tell him to look up.' As I said this, his guardian angel opened up. The guardian angel gave a strong masculine appearance and was dressed in red and gold. He was standing, bent fully over the man, like a bendy toy, as if in a sense looking at his face (I know we can't do this humanly, so it's a little hard to imagine).

The guardian angel straightened up as I said hello and the man lifted his head and acknowledged me.

The tables were arranged in long rows and I sat at a table for two near the wall. The man was in the next row of tables several tables away, facing me. He looked over at me and I could see him properly for the first time. He was in his forties and well dressed, but his eyes were red. His guardian angel told me I was to ask him how he was. I did so and, for a long time, he just looked at me without saying a word. I repeated my question. This time he got up from his table and approached me, carrying his mug of coffee with him. He didn't join me at my table, but sat at the next one to me. He told me that he wasn't OK. He said that his mother had died some weeks before, and that it wasn't until she was dying that he realised just how little he knew her.

I let him talk without interrupting; he talked about 'those six short weeks where I learnt so much about her'. It was as if he hadn't known her before. He hadn't appreciated that his mother had a life; that she had friends of different ages and from different walks of life, and that she had interests she shared with these friends – he knew nothing of that. He told me that he was so sad that he hadn't known the woman she was with these friends;

that he hadn't taken the time to learn what interested her, and participate in these interests with her. He told me that it was only over this 'six weeks' that he realised just how much he loved her.

He talked and I listened. He continued to speak freely. I could see his guardian angel leaning over him and I know that this angel was helping him to express what he was feeling, that he was helping him to overcome any inhibitions that he had concerning talking in this way to a stranger.

After about twenty minutes, he told me he had better get going. I wished him well.

I know he will never forget those precious 'six weeks' when his eyes were opened to his mum as a person in her own right, not just as his mother. As long as they are still alive, it's never too late to reach out and get to know your parents as people. Remember you chose your parents before you were conceived. You chose them knowing their strengths and their weaknesses. As a baby, you loved them unconditionally.

I was challenged about this on a visit to an Irish prison. I had been invited to speak to a group of women prisoners. We were in an open area, with some of the prison guards and the place was full of angels. I was talking about how we all choose our parents. There was a woman prisoner standing, leaning against the wall. An angel appeared in front of her and walked towards me; she gave a female appearance and was dressed in a yellowish-green colour. She had her two hands out at chest level, with the palms facing me. 'Lorna, this is a hard one!' the angel said.

I took a deep breath, knowing I would need courage and strength as the woman burst out at me in a strong voice: '*No way* could I have chosen my mother! She used to stub out cigarettes on me; she was drunk all the time and let me go hungry. I hated her! How could I possibly have chosen her to be my mum, I'd have to have been mad to have chosen her.'

There was a compassionate and shocked silence in the room. I struggled for words; no child should ever have to experience something like that, and there is no excuse for it at all. But the angel dressed in yellowish-green was there, telling me that despite what the woman was saying, she did love her mother; and her mother, regardless of her appalling behaviour, loved her daughter. The mother was an addict and didn't know how to show love for herself, let alone her child.

I can't remember exactly what I said to the woman. I know that my answer felt inadequate to me, but the chaplain, Father John, said I did give her food for thought, and it did help her to change the way she thought about her mother.

The truth is that, as I say, we do choose our parents, and we choose them knowing all about them, their weaknesses and strengths, and the choices they face. I have no idea why one would choose a mother like that, but I do know that in our lives here on earth we all have choices to make. This mother had the choice to over-come her addiction and to look after her daughter properly; and the daughter had the choice – and continues to have the choice – not to allow what had happened to her as a child to destroy her own life.

So often I come across situations where relationships with parents are destroyed, or damaged for many years, because of misunderstandings.

I had been married for quite a long time before we got a telephone in our cottage in Maynooth, and then we only got it because my husband Joe might need to see a doctor urgently. Very occasionally strangers used to ring me looking for help; I never knew where they got my number from, or who had sent them.

One evening, when I was pregnant with my youngest child, Megan, the phone rang. When I answered there was a woman who told me her name was Lesley and that she was ringing from London. An angel appeared beside me and indicated that I should give her some time.

I stood in the kitchen holding the phone as Lesley started talking. She told me that ten years earlier when she was in her early twenties, she had left her home in Mayo to live in London. She said that she had never had a good relationship with her parents and had always felt that they favoured her younger brother and sister over her. She felt they didn't love her, and so she couldn't wait for an opportunity to get away from them.

When she was in London she lost all contact with her parents. Her mother would write to her, but she would never reply. Occasionally her sister would write to her, and about once a year she would reply to her sister, but always made a point of not enquiring about her parents in the letter, let alone send them her love. As far as she was concerned, there was no connection between her parents and herself.

She told me that eight months previously she had received a wedding invitation from her sister. With it came a note from her sister begging her to come to her wedding, saying how much she wanted Lesley to be there to meet her new husband and that her parents loved Lesley and wanted her to be there too.

Lesley had ignored the invitation; she didn't even bother to reply. By now Lesley was sobbing at the other end of the phone as she told me that just a week earlier she had received photos from her sister of her wedding, and beautiful photos of the whole family. With them came a letter from her sister describing how their parents had cried on her wedding day because Lesley wasn't there, and how they loved her and missed her.

The angel with me told me that her parents had always loved her, and that they hadn't favoured her younger brother and sister over her, but that Lesley, as the oldest child, had felt hard done by, through being asked to share things with her younger siblings.

Lesley told me that she was so ashamed of all those years when she had refused to have any contact with her mother; that her heart was aching at the idea that her parents had cried on her sister's wedding day because she was too stubborn to even consider going to the wedding.

She told me that she wanted to make contact

with her parents, but that she was very afraid to. The angel told me to tell Lesley to ring her mum and dad and to assure her that they were waiting for her call; that they had been waiting and praying for it for ten years since she went to London. I also told her that the angel had told me that they loved her very much.

I said a prayer for her as we finished the call. I prayed that she had the courage to take the first step and make the call. I knew from what the angels had told me that her parents were waiting with open arms for this longstanding misunderstanding to be resolved.

Don't wait to resolve misunderstandings with your parents. If you have differences, take the steps to resolve them. I meet far too many people who fail to do this and then regret it when it is too late.

So often, problems with parents come from a feeling a person has that that parent may have loved them less than their brothers or sisters.

I remember being in the hospital visiting her when my husband's mother Liz was dying. She was in the same ward for about six weeks so I got to know some of the patients and recognise their families. There was an elderly woman in the bed on the other side of the ward. The first time I was in the ward she was on her own, and I could see her guardian angel standing at the head of the bed behind her, holding her soul with great compassion. I knew from this that her guardian angel would shortly be taking her home to heaven.

The next time I visited she was surrounded by four middle-aged adults. I could see the circular thread connecting her and them, so I knew they were her children. An angel told me to look at the family carefully, so I tried to do this without being noticed. As I looked, one of the daughters moved and I could see that in addition to the circular thread going around all the family, there was an additional thread going from the mother to this particular daughter. This thread was darker in colour. The angel told me it was there to help to strengthen the love bond between this daughter and the mother. The mother had loved all her children equally as children, but for some reason the bond with this particular child had got weaker over time. The angels told me that the mother really wanted, before she died, for her daughter to know she had loved her. God had allowed this extra thread in order to help the daughter to feel her mother's love.

I was in the ward once more when the family were with their mother, and I could still see this additional cord between the woman and this daughter. The cord was a much brighter colour this time, almost as if it was lit up by the love that was flowing between them. I smiled to myself and said to the angels, 'I think it's working, I hope it does.'

Often when a parent is dying, sons or daughters can feel a great rush of love for their parent, alongside a great sadness – and it can feel devastating.

Many people find themselves aware that they never told their parents that they loved them; that they never had the courage to say the words 'I love you'.

Don't presume that your parents know that

you love them; you need to tell them – you need to say the words.

Don't wait until it's too late.

Of course, if your parent has already gone home to heaven, you can still tell them now and they will hear you.

The experience of having a parent (or anyone close to you) with Alzheimer's disease or dementia can be profoundly upsetting.

One woman I knew, called Maeve, spoke to me about it. Her mother, who lived with her, her husband and their three teenage children, had started to get confused. Sometimes she didn't even know them. Maeve described how one afternoon her mother had shouted at her grandson when he came in from school; she accused him of being a robber and told him to get out of her house. When he tried to reassure his granny and calm her down, she hit him with her walking stick. As she told me this, Maeve's guardian angel opened up. It gave a female appearance and was dressed in gold and white. She was wrapped around Maeve, as if enveloping her in a protective cocoon. This guardian angel told me that Maeve would soon have to let her mother go into a nursing home; that this would be the right thing to do, and that her mum would be safe and happy there.

Maeve was so stressed and worried about the situation; she wanted to do the right thing for her mother, and also for her husband and their children. She told me that it felt as if her heart was being ripped out.

 Don't presume that your parents know that you love them; you need to tell them – you need to say the words 'I love you'.

As her mother's mind deteriorated, Maeve became more and more afraid for her mother. Eventually she made the decision to place her mother in a nursing home. Maeve spoke to me about it some months after her mother had settled into the home. She said her mother was doing well and seemed content. Maeve's guardian angel told me that her mother was comfortable, but that on some occasions she got a little upset as she didn't know who the strangers sitting by her bed were, and wondered when her daughter and grandchildren would come to visit.

I have no idea why people get Alzheimer's disease and dementia, but I know that their guardian angels are with them all the time, doing their best to help and protect them. I know that as it comes nearer to their time to go home, the guardian angel will be holding on to the soul of that person, and at the moment of death they will know and remember everything and everyone.

I met one man who told me that his father had dementia and because he had found it so hard to see him in this state, he had stopped going to visit him. He hadn't seen him for three years, entrusting his care to professionals. I gently suggested that just because his father didn't recognise him didn't mean he didn't love him, and that he should get up the courage to go and visit his father. I said a prayer that he would conquer his fears and go.

Even if he just sat by his father's bed reading the newspaper, his presence is important. I know that if this man doesn't find the courage to visit, he will regret it deeply after his father dies.

When my father died I was devastated and I still miss him today. I was in my late thirties and married with children when it happened, and I can't even begin to imagine the pain of losing a parent early in one's life.

Our parents, though, while they may be in heaven are with us when we need them. Most days, if I am out and about, I see at least one person with the soul of a parent who has already gone to heaven with them. This soul is still in heaven, but is allowed by God to be with loved ones when they need help or support. When I see a soul I am shown a faint human form, with light radiating from it. I see them around a son or daughter, talking into their ear or touching their arm in support. Strange as it may seem, it is easier for us to feel the presence of a soul than it is the presence of our guardian angel, or another angel, and this is one of the reasons why our guardian angels often let in the soul of a parent, or another loved one who is in heaven, to help us.

At one book signing a woman in her mid-fifties told me how her mother had died when she was seven years old. She told me she could still remember her mum wiping her face clean with a wet handkerchief after she had eaten jam sandwiches. As she talked about her mother, her mother's soul appeared – standing beside her. Her mother looked so beautiful, as she must have done in her prime, and looked like a younger version of her daughter who was sitting down talking with me.

'Your mum is in and around you, she is there when you need her. I'm sure you feel it at times,' I said, not telling the daughter what I was seeing. The daughter nodded. 'I'm sure you look very like your mum did,' I added.

She looked up at me and said, 'Everyone says that.'

'Your mum is with you, every time you think

or talk about her,' I said to her as I gave her a goodbye hug. It was beautiful to see the strength of the love that had lasted almost fifty years and the way this woman kept her few precious memories of her mother alive inside of her.

Occasionally someone will tell me that they had a really bad relationship with a parent who is now dead. When someone dies, all of these differences are washed away; all the human imperfections that lead to rows and anger disappear and the soul of the parent simply feels pure love for children who are left behind.

Don't be afraid to talk to them. You can ask a parent, or any soul, to intercede with God for you, to help with anything in your life. I still miss my da, but I draw enormous comfort from the fact that he is in heaven, asking God and his angels to help me and my family.

Recently I visited the Czech Republic and Slovakia. When I was on the plane, the angels with me told me that I would experience something that would touch my heart. But they wouldn't tell me anything more.

I was halfway through blessing more than a thousand people in the beautiful Lucerna Hall in Prague when I suddenly realised what it was. There were a lot of young people, sometimes in groups, coming up to be blessed, but what was so unusual was how many of these young people were asking me, often in broken English, to give the blessing for their parents, not for them. This has happened occasionally before, but never in such big numbers.

One young man of about seventeen said to me, with tears in his eyes, 'My parents are so stressed and I would like this blessing for them. I would love my parents to be happy.'

The young man's guardian angel was behind him, holding on to him, and it told me to look into the boy's eyes. I did so and could see so much love shining from them. This boy loved his parents deeply and really hoped that this blessing could help to bring more joy into their life together. I said a prayer that it would as I blessed him.

I was very touched by the number of young people being so concerned about their parents.

It was as if these youngsters appreciated what was going on in their parents' lives, as if much more was shared. They knew their parents more fully as individuals, and this awareness was deepening their love.

I have no explanation for why I encountered this so often in the Czech Republic and Slovakia, perhaps it had something to do with the recent history of these countries. All I know is I would like to see more heartfelt love and appreciation for parents across the world.

CHAPTER SEVEN

Love of animals

I HAVE ALWAYS LOVED ANIMALS, AND AS I write this I am the proud owner of a rabbit who has a phantom pregnancy, two canaries, a little dog called Holly who can't walk very well, and I have just been asked to give a home to twenty laying hens. Animals have always been an important part of my life.

As a child of seven or eight I spent a lot of time on my own and often the angels would play animal hide-and-seek with me, and have me playing as if looking for an animal. The angels would give me clues, a little movement of grass, the sound of a leaf breaking, or a fish jumping in the water. Sometimes a bird would fly out of the grass and fly low and slow so I could follow and catch up.

One particular afternoon the angels didn't play hide-and-seek with me, but instead told me to run quickly – that there was an animal that needed me. The angels showed me the way. When I got near to where they wanted me to go, they told me to walk slowly and quietly. I did so and there underneath a clump of bushes I could see a rabbit surrounded by six angels who were touching it and calming it. It had got its foot entangled in a piece of wire fencing that had been discarded, and it was now stuck. The animal was very scared and I approached it very carefully, terrified it would die of fright. The angels kept it calm as I reached out and stroked it and talked gently to it.

It was really hard to get the rabbit's foot out of the wire, and I asked God and the angels to help me. The wire was scratching me and I had cuts all over my hand by the time I eventually got the rabbit free.

The rabbit hopped some distance away from where it had been trapped and then turned and looked back at me for a moment before it ran away. I was so happy that it was free. I had freed the animal out of kindness, but the angels with me that day told me that what we sometimes call 'kindness' is in fact 'love'.

I saw this more clearly a few years later when I was in the country with my da. There was a small village with a river where we often went to fish, and I had got to know some of the farmers nearby. There was one woman who I always thought of as old. I realise now that she probably wasn't that old, but she always wore an apron and had her hair in a perm. She seemed very cross and I never saw any kindness in her, although the angels assured me that she was a kind woman.

One day I rounded the barn in her yard and just at the door of the barn I saw her pick up a little kitten, and as I did I saw the force of love come from her towards the kitten. It was as if her heart opened and all the love she had bottled up there flowed out. I saw blood on her hand and realised that the kitten was injured in some way.

The angels with me said, 'We told you she was a kind woman.' They continued, 'She never wants anyone to see that part of her, because she thinks that love makes her vulnerable and open to being hurt, but when she saw the injured kitten she couldn't control the love inside of her, it just poured out of her.'

Just after the angels said this, the woman saw me and said sharply, 'What are you doing here?' I ignored the question and moved towards her, enquiring about the kitten.

She looked down at the kitten rather dismissively, saying, 'I'm just being kind, doing what anyone would do with an injured animal.' She trivialised her feelings; but the angels told me that kindness is love.

It's important that we all realise that kindness is love. If we are more kind, and allow more of our love out, we can change so much in our world.

When I was newly married and living in Maynooth, I would sometimes see an elderly man who always carried a bundle of sticks. He was always closely followed on his left-hand side by a big black dog with a stick in its mouth. The dog for some reason *always* walked on his left-hand side. Like the man, the dog was getting on in years, and I could see that at times they both had difficulties moving.

 The angels have told me that kindness is love.

I could see the force of love pouring out from this man to the dog. It was very powerful and came not just from his hand or a part of him; it came from every bit of him. I know lots of people love their animals, but I don't often see love for an animal flowing with this intensity. The dog could feel the depth of the love from the man which was why it kept so close, stuck like glue to the old man.

I saw the old man lying asleep on the grass on the other side of the canal one day as I walked to the shops. The dog was lying beside him, resting his head on the old man's knee. I was really surprised to see the force of love coming from the man to the dog even as the man slept. It is very rare to see the force of love coming from any human who is asleep; I have only seen it on a few special occasions. This man's love for his dog was so intense that he was pouring it out to the dog constantly, twenty-four hours a day.

I was going to walk back from the shops the shorter way as I was carrying shopping, but Angel Hosus told me I needed to walk along the canal again. The old man and the dog were still sleeping where they had been, but were now surrounded by angels.

Angel Hosus told me that it was time the old man woke up, that it wasn't good for him to be sleeping so long on the hard ground. As he said this to me, one of the angels reached down and started to stroke the dog; the animal woke for a moment, lifted its head, and then gently started to lick the man awake.

I was looking at something else, though

– something I had never noticed before, and didn't fully understand. I turned to Angel Hosus and said, 'That fine mist I am seeing coming from the dog to the man. Is that the force of love?' Hosus nodded. I had never seen that coming from an animal to a human before 'How is it possible for an animal to love a human like that?' I wondered.

Let me explain a little about the differences in the way that animals and humans love. We humans are pure love and are able to give a tremendous amount of love, if we don't lock too much of it away. Human love can change the world.

Most of the love that comes from an animal is human love reflected back. When you look into the eyes of an animal you love, you see love. It is the love you have lavished on the animal being reflected back to you.

There is enormous comfort in this reflected love, but it is different from human love and less intense.

The only time I have ever seen the love from an animal as a physical force was with this old man and his dog, and I know this was because the old man was pouring love out on to his dog not only in his waking hours, but twenty-four hours a day.

The dog licked the man's face and the man slowly woke up; he then got up and walked towards me on the other bank of the canal. The man gave me a little wave and the dog turned its head to look at me as they passed. For several years after that I would see them occasionally, and I always looked for, and saw, this force of love going from the dog to the man; it was so special to see.

Animals are very sensitive and will feel our emotions more than many people will. This is why a loved pet will come and sit with you when you're sad or down, offering tremendous consolation. This sometimes makes people feel that their pet understands them more than the people in their lives. Pets are a gift from God and they give great pleasure and contribute greatly to our lives.

Our pets don't challenge us, which is one of the reasons they are such a joy to be with. None of us is perfect; I'm not perfect, nor you, nor anyone around us. This is why human relationships come with challenges. We should not, though, confuse the loyalty and affection of a pet with human love.

From the age of about twelve, I used to walk past a small house where there was a yellow Labrador retriever. This dog would always be out waiting for his owner – a young man – to come home. I watched this over a number of years. Initially the boy was coming home from school, and then he was coming home from work or college. Sometimes I would see the young man out in the small front garden rolling around on the grass, playing with the dog. There was so much friendship between them.

Then one day the dog wasn't there. I had no idea what had happened. I asked the angels but got no answer, and for about a week or so I saw no dog and knew nothing more.

Then one day I was passing and the young man was sitting on the grass in the front garden on his own, surrounded by angels. The angels with me told me to walk slowly. The angels surrounding the young man were consoling him, and I knew for sure that the dog had died. It made me sad, and I didn't even know the dog's name, but I knew the young man was heartbroken.

As he sat there, an angel walked towards him and, with him, was the ghost of his dog. Animals don't have souls, but the angels have told me that if we really love an animal, and it has been an important part of our life, then God will have the animal there in heaven waiting for us. The young man, of course, couldn't see the ghost of the dog. I said a little prayer that the young man would feel the presence of the dog, or feel its touch, and would know that it was there for him.

The angels with me told me that his guardian angel would allow the ghost of his dog to be in and around him at those times he most needed support and help.

I know some people find it hard to believe that animals don't have souls. But they don't! I can only tell you what I have seen and been told by God and the angels. God has given each of us – every man, woman and child – a soul.

God hasn't given any animal a soul. I have no idea why, and I know it will disappoint some of you, but I can only tell what I have been told. Even if someone really loves a pet, the animal won't develop a soul.

Angels help animals, but no animal has a guardian angel. We have been given guardian angels because we have souls; our guardian angels are the gatekeepers of our souls. I do see angels helping animals, but I don't see them in anything like the abundance that I see them with people. If I look over a gate, for example, I probably won't see any angels in a field of cows. When I see angels with animals, it normally indicates that we either need to help the animal, or that the animal is in danger from humans.

As a child, the angels would let me see things like a fox catching a rabbit for food. The angels wouldn't interfere in situations like this. They would tell me that the fox needed the food to feed its young. I have never been told by the angels not to eat meat. Indeed, as a child at my Granny's, the angels would tell me that the pigs were being fattened up to be eaten. I remember being eight and looking at a rasher on my plate, asking if it was one of the pigs I knew. They assured me it wasn't.

Animals may not have individual guardian angels, but angels do help to protect them and call on us to be the guardian angels of animals. I was recently at the riding stables where my daughter Ruth rides and helps out. I was leaning against the car which was parked by the paddock, waiting for Ruth. There were about twenty angels outside of the paddock rails. They weren't doing anything other than standing there, looking at a man saddling up his horse in the paddock. With the man were another four angels. To be honest, I didn't give any of these angels much thought.

I saw Ruth and Anne, who owns the riding stables, lead a beautiful horse from the stable. There were several angels with them and they kept whispering to the girls. They girls were chatting and laughing and every so often the girls would stop moving. When they stopped, I would see one of the angels put its hand on the horse as if it was encouraging it to move towards the paddock.

I got a shock when suddenly all the angels surrounding the paddock rail jumped over the railings. They were accompanied by a breeze, which made Ruth and Anne look towards the centre of the paddock. As they did, the man who was standing in the paddock with the horse started to whip it with a ferocity and anger that was shocking.

The man was surrounded by angels who were whispering to him, but they couldn't get him to listen, and were not physically able to intervene without human help. Anne ran towards the man, roaring as she ran, 'Stop that! No one is going to beat a horse in my stable.' She climbed over the fence and ran to the centre of the paddock, grabbing the whip from the man.

The horse was surrounded by angels trying to calm it as Anne took its reins and walked the horse away, all the time talking quietly to it. She called Ruth to bring the other horse into the paddock, so its presence would help to soothe the poor horse who had been beaten.

I never learnt what was going on that had made the man treat his horse with such cruelty; Ruth tells me he no longer comes to Anne's stables, but I know that the angels were working hard to protect the horse that day.

Cruelty to animals is unacceptable in any circumstances; we are all called upon to watch out for occasions where animals are being mistreated and to then act. We are called upon to act as guardian angels for all animals, not just pets.

Soon after Megan and I had moved to Johnstown, and were still working on the house, an elderly man came to see me. I have no idea how he knew I was there, but he parked on the lane and walked into what was basically a building site. He was small and round and used a walking stick, and was surrounded by angels. As he approached me, the light of his guardian angel opened up and I could see that it was holding on to his soul. His guardian angel was looking down at him with huge compassion. I needed no one to tell me that it was very near his time.

After a little chat about the building work – I discovered this man had known the old farmhouse in the time of a previous owner – the man got up the courage to tell me why he was *really* there. He told me that he knew he was dying and was very afraid. His guardian angel told me he had no one else to share his fears with.

His guardian angel asked me to ask him whether he had ever had a pet that he loved dearly. I did, and he told me that he had a dog, a collie called Rex, for many years and that he had loved the dog very much. He said, 'Rex died in my arms two years ago. I wish he was here for me now in my hour of need.'

I asked him if he ever felt Rex around him. As I asked this, an angel appeared with a beautiful brown and cream collie. The angel then put its finger up to its mouth, indicating that I shouldn't tell the man the dog was there.

The man looked at me strangely and said, 'I think I hear Rex sometimes. He never liked having his nails clipped, so I would delay taking him to the vet. I hear his scratchy way of walking near me sometimes.'

His guardian angel told me to tell him that God had Rex in heaven waiting for him, and that Rex was there to comfort him when he needed him.

The man left looking so much happier, knowing he would see his beloved collie again.

If you have, or have had, a pet that has been an important part of your life and that you really loved, God will have it waiting in heaven for you too.

CHAPTER EIGHT

Love of children

EACH GENERATION OF HUMANITY IS INTENDED to be more loving than the previous one. This is God's plan for our evolution. The only way that this evolution can happen as it should is for our children to be more loving and compassionate than we are. The angels tell me that this has been happening for generations, but that this evolution has slowed down in the last two generations. I am shown that children are in danger of becoming more cold-hearted instead of more loving in the next generation. And it will be *our* fault!

Children (and remember teenagers are still children) are watching and learning from adults all the time. As our world has become more materialistic and less compassionate, children are not seeing enough love in their own families, in communities, and in our world as a whole. We are living in the twenty-first century. We have seen so many advances in many areas, and yet where I live in Ireland we have children going to school hungry, children homeless, children deprived of psychiatric services, or disadvantaged in education. In the wider world we have children starving, dying of curable diseases, being killed in unnecessary wars. Is it any wonder that children seeing adults acting as if this is normal and acceptable are becoming cold-hearted?

It's possible to let this situation overwhelm us, to decide it's such a big problem that we can't as individuals do anything about it, so let me suggest three things the angels have told me that each and every one of us can do, and need to do, as individuals:

- Spend more quality time with children.
- Be an example to children.
- Stand up for children and demand that our government, leaders and international institutions do the right thing by children, and hold these authorities to account if they don't.

'Dad, if I give you the money in my piggybank, will you spend some time with me?' A father I met told me that he was horrified when his seven-year-old son asked him this. He was so shocked and ashamed that his son thought he needed to pay him to spend time with him. It gave him a wake-up call, though, and the father told me that in the two years since this had happened, he had changed a lot of things in his life to allow him to spend more time with his children.

The angels are telling me that we adults have become more preoccupied and focused on our own fulfilment. Children have become less important in our world and we are spending less time with them.

This isn't just about parents, it's about everyone. We all need to make a conscious effort to spend more time with children. We need to stop and talk to children who we encounter in our daily lives, to do our best to get to know the names and interests of the neighbourhood children. We all have talents, interests and hobbies, and we need to share these interests and enthusiasm with children around us.

We are not engaging enough with children of all ages – from very young ones to teenagers. Young children are learning to communicate and it's very important that we give them the time to develop this ability. When young children want to talk, we need to stop what we are doing and listen to them in a focused way, giving them all the time they need.

Many people fear engaging with teenagers. They fear the young people's anger or ridicule, and sometimes are afraid of them physically. The angels are telling me that teenagers of today are more isolated than in any previous generation. This is a result of not enough time with family, too much time on social media, and the reluctance and fear of many adults to engage with them.

Teenagers need our respect, and our engagement. They are looking at the world, and much of the time it seems to them to be an incomprehensible place. We need to talk with them and give them the time and opportunity to explore things. There is so much joy in spending time with young people; and when we fail to do this, we deprive both ourselves and them.

> **If we don't help the children in our world, the cost will be incalculable, and will be paid for by future generations of humanity.**

The angels tell me that children and teenagers today are seeing less kindness and love from adults, and more selfishness and nastiness. If this is the example they are being shown, how can they grow up into caring and loving people?

All adults need to be aware that they are role models for children and young people.

Children look up to their parents and expect them to be role models, but far too few parents are conscious of this. Frequently they are poor role models, even if they are trying to do their best. Far too often children fill this gap by looking to 'celebrities' to provide them with role models. As children get access to more media and at a younger age, this is happening more and more. Most of these role models are based around being more successful, famous, better looking and wealthier than others. They create a set of expectations for children that few lives will live up to, and often provide a bad example. Children need to identify with role models within their wider families or communities – people who are living loving and fulfilled lives, full of different passions and joy.

Every time we do something – offering someone a seat on a bus, smiling at someone, cursing a driver who we think has cut in on us, or making a racial slur – we are providing an example for children. We need to be more conscious of this and ask ourselves whether we are providing a good example for future generations.

I am enormously frustrated at the lack of progress that the world has made in relation to children. Children are unable to stand up for themselves, so we have to stand up for them. We have failed them. How can we live with ourselves when we still have children dying of hunger, dying of curable diseases, working as slaves, being killed in unnecessary wars? The angels are telling me we are so far behind where we are supposed to be because we have handed authority over to people who are putting power and money before doing the right thing for children.

God and the angels have been showing me the terror of many of these children. I have been allowed to feel the pain and the suffering they are experiencing and their feelings of help-lessness and hopelessness when no one comes to help them. Imagine that this was one of your children – that you weren't able to help them, and no one else did. They just allowed your child to suffer.

And yet we don't stand up and demand that the world do something to stop so much unnecessary horror and suffering among children.

There are some people who *do* stand up, speak out, and do try to change things, but they are too few and the rest of us are not giving them nearly enough support. Too often the appeals of such people fall on deaf ears, or they will be told that it doesn't make economic sense to make a particular change. Let me assure you that any decisions in relation to children that are primarily made on economic costs are wrong. If we don't help the children in our world, the cost will be incalculable, and will be paid for by future generations of humanity. You can imagine what sort of adults these children, who have suffered while the world looked on and did nothing, will become.

We need to grow up and get our priorities right. We each have a choice to make. Do we love the children of the world? This is not a wishy-washy question and decision. If we love children, we need to stand up and act. We need to play our part and make sure that our governments and international institutions do the right thing; and that if they don't, they must be held accountable.

CHAPTER NINE

Making the conscious decision to love your own life

THE YOUNG WOMAN WALKED ALONG THE street on her way back to work after her lunch. From every part of her burst a fine mist that was transparent in colour, but seemed to be electrified with tiny silver sparks. The force with which it was coming from her was so strong that at times it reached more than three feet out from her, surrounding her like a very fine bubble. This mist seemed to be energising her physically and mentally; as I walked towards her, with the angel with no name a little behind me, I could see that the mist seemed to clear her mind, like a breath of fresh air, allowing her to think clearly.

As I walked past the girl, I brushed the mist and was allowed to feel it on my bare arm for a split second. It felt a little like pins and needles, but was very pleasant.

This energy was not love, but was what I would call love-of-life. This girl really loved her life and was fully awake to all that was going on around her. There was nothing she wanted to do more in the whole world at that moment than walk down that street and go back to work.

The angel with no name told me that this energy wasn't there because something special was happening at work that afternoon, or that she was doing her 'dream job' – she wasn't. It was there because she had got into the habit of loving all the little everyday ordinary things that were happening in her life.

Coming from her, quite separate and different

from her love-of-life, I could see her love for herself. It flowed more gently and slowly than the other energy I was seeing, and had more substance than the fine mist of energy linked to her love-of-life. Her love for herself came out from her and then doubled back like a wave to flow over her.

This young woman loved herself, *and* she loved her life.

Very few of us love life enough; very few of us love it to the extent that this girl does. Most of us allow small things to get in the way of our enjoyment of life, and we get into the habit of not seeing all the wonderful things that are in our lives. I see this bad habit start at a very early age. When I see a young child who is not getting their own way, I will sometimes see them suck in the love-of-life energy. It doesn't normally last long with a young child, though, and within a few minutes I will see this energy burst forward again.

As an adult, if we are not used to letting this energy burst forward, it may take us a little longer to remember how to do it. The more conscious you become of loving life, the more you build up this energy, which helps you physically and mentally.

It is important to bring love-of-life to the work you are doing – whatever it is. You don't have to love the job – it may be far short of what you aspire to – but when you approach it with love-of-life, you will be able to enjoy it, do a good job, and make the best of any opportunities it brings.

When I was going through Zurich Airport recently the angels brought my attention to two young men who were working as airport cleaners. I was going up an escalator and they came down in the opposite direction, cleaning the escalator as they went. From one of them I could see the energy of love-of life flow. From the other there was nothing, and one of the angels with him told me that in fact he was embarrassed to be a cleaner, and hated the work. The man who was enjoying his work was doing all he could to help his colleague. They were speaking German, but the angels with them told me that this is what their chat was about. Next to the young man who was unhappy in the job was a teacher angel. He had a cleaning cloth in one hand and was helping him physically in his work. He was also doing his best, without much success, to get this young man to smile.

When you approach work or any task with love-of-life, the task becomes so much easier, you gain more confidence, and start to see the positives in the work you are doing. You realise how much you enjoy your colleagues, or how nice so many of the customers are, or you simply appreciate going home with a pay-packet. When you approach work with this love-of-life you have more mental and physical energy and are able to do a better job. You are open to see and seize opportunities to learn new things, or take on a new job. It helps to move you forward in life. People who really love life are frequently not in the most important jobs. They may not need as much as others need in terms of stimulation, or reward, but they often, though, live much more satisfying and happier work lives than those who seek a 'higher status'.

About four years ago I was driving from Maynooth to Nass, some 25 miles from my home. A young man was thumbing a lift and there was an angel standing beside him. I rarely give strangers lifts, but Angel Hosus who was beside me in the car told me to stop. I did as he asked. I wound down the window and told the young man where I was going, and he got in. He hadn't said a word, not even hello, and he sat there in silence. I had driven for about ten minutes when the angel with him asked me to talk to him. I asked him whether Nass was far enough, as I wasn't going further. In a very depressed voice he said, 'It makes no difference where you drop me off.' Nothing more. I was getting very uncomfortable and nervous about this young man, and when the angel told me to stop as soon as I could I was happy to do so. I turned into a supermarket parking area about halfway to Nass. He looked up. 'Are you only going this far?' he asked. 'I thought you said you were going to Nass.'

I looked at him and replied, 'I thought you said it didn't matter!'

The boy shouted at me, 'Nothing matters! What's the point in living, nothing is happening for me.' He started to cry. His guardian angel opened for one second and embraced him. I sat there silently while his guardian angel and the other angel gently encouraged him to keep talking to me. Eventually he did.

'I did business studies in college; I got my degree and then had a job for a few years,' he said. 'I was made redundant and now I can't find any work.' The angel with him told me what to say. 'When did you last enjoy life?' I asked.

He looked at me as if I had two heads, but he did take a few moments before he replied. 'I enjoyed school and college, I suppose,' he said. I asked him if he had enjoyed work and he nodded. The angel with him kept on telling me what to say, so much so that I had to work hard to keep up with this angel. It told me to tell the young man that he needed to remember how much he enjoyed college and work when he went looking for a job. That it didn't matter what the job he did was, but that he needed to do something and to remember how he had enjoyed working in the past. The most important things that the angel kept telling me to repeat in different words were that he needed to remember the times when he had felt the energy of love-of-life and to bring that positivity into his life now.

I said all I was asked to say and then I drove him on to Nass and dropped him off where he asked me to. I had no idea if he had listened or not, but to be honest I was worried about what would happen to him if he didn't recover his love-of-life, and I prayed often for him in the following months.

About a year ago I stopped at a hotel for coffee to break up my car journey. An angel told me to walk through the lobby on my way out. I did as I was asked and became conscious of someone following me. At the door another angel told me to slow down. I did, and a young man came up to me. He asked me if I remembered him; I shook my head to say no. It was the young man – who was now working in this hotel. I would never have recognised him; he looked so happy and I could see that fine mist of energy of love-of-life coming from him. He said he never thought he'd see me again, and just wanted to thank me for reminding him to recall the times he had loved life.

I was thrilled to see him, and so happy that he had listened.

Enjoying life is a decision we all need to make, no matter how rough things may seem. You have to make a *conscious* decision to love life. It won't happen on its own and no one else can do it for you. One way to help you to become conscious of your own love-of-life is to do as this young man did, and remember the times you felt it in your own life.

Like him, many people have got into the habit of not loving life. I don't think it happens deliberately, but it seems to be a habit that comes easily to us. It's a habit, though, that has a seriously destructive effect on our lives, and erodes so much of our potential for happiness. We need to break this habit by starting to see the little joys that are in our lives. I meet mothers who see their lives as one chore after another, and forget to see all the moments when they really love being a mother. When we allow ourselves to love life we get energised mentally and physically, and start to see more purpose in our lives. We become happier and healthier people, more able to cope with whatever life throws at us. We become more compassionate and loving, less judgemental.

I am not just talking about enjoying the 'high points', the special events, the holidays, the weekends. I am talking about enjoying each and every moment of the day because our life is made up of the ordinary things. There are not enough 'high points' in a life to make someone truly happy. And anyway, 'high points' can become routine and boring in turn, and then new highs continually need to be sought.

If we get into the habit of enjoying life, and seeing the good things there, it is easier to lift ourselves out of a blue period. The physical and mental vibrancy that comes from enjoying life will give you a resilience to help you move forward when you are feeling down or depressed.

Often when I am in Dublin I will go into Clarendon Street Church off Grafton Street to say a short prayer. A few months ago when I was in there I noticed a young man sitting a few rows away from me. The reason I noticed him was that his beautiful guardian angel who had opened was a little bit closer to him than guardian angels normally are. This angel was showing the young man so much love.

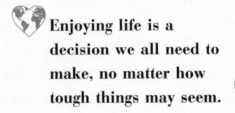 **Enjoying life is a decision we all need to make, no matter how tough things may seem.**

The angel looked over at me and asked me to pray for the young man. A short while later the young man looked in my direction and caught my eye; I gave him a smile. He got up and came over and sat beside me. He said he knew who I was and asked if he could speak to me for a few minutes. He told me he was very unhappy and had completely lost his love for life. He spoke of an ex-girlfriend who was getting married – to someone else. This upset him, but what made him really upset and fearful was that he was afraid that when she married, he would see less of their five-year-old daughter whom he loved dearly. We talked for a bit.

His guardian angel, who remained open all the time, asked me to ask him whether he had anyone else in his life. He looked at me and replied that he had a girlfriend, who he had met shortly after he and his ex-girlfriend had broken up, and that they had now been together for three years. He didn't seem to get any joy from having a girlfriend; he was so consumed with fear that he would lose his daughter, and this was tinged with jealousy that his ex-girlfriend was getting married.

He said goodbye and got up; I could see that he was still very down. I was told to stay there, praying. Something very beautiful then happened. A band of angels shaped like a V walked down the church towards him. There were six angels in each arm of the V; they all looked the same, bright white and very tall, with pointy wings that were full of light. The

V was perfectly formed and seemed to glow with each angel walking in the light of the other angels.

The angels surrounded him as he sat down again to say another little prayer. A few minutes later he turned and looked at me and gave me a big smile. I asked his guardian angel what had happened. He told me that it was as if suddenly he had seen not just solutions, but opportunities. The conversation with me, and the intervention of the angels, had made him realise he loved his new girlfriend, and it wasn't just his ex-girlfriend who had a chance of happiness. He had suddenly lost much of his fear of losing his daughter, and was starting to believe that these changes might not be so bad. Now I could see his love-of-life coming from him – it wasn't a full burst, and only came out a few inches, but he was seeing much more of the positives within his life.

We all need to be reminded to enjoy life. Teenagers in particular need to be reminded. I get frustrated when people tell me they won't try something as they think it will be boring.

We all need to try new things and go into them expecting to enjoy them, seeking to find aspects that we do enjoy.

I'm enjoying writing this despite the fact that I am writing against a deadline. The angels have trained me from the time I was a child to feel joy and energy regardless of what I am doing. Even when I have aches and pains or am worried about something, the angels tell me that I need to enjoy life.

Lots of people feel called to take on a cause that other people might regard as a burden. Very often their commitment to this cause feeds their love of life and this in turn energises and empowers them to overcome hurdles and barriers that might be put in their way.

There was a lovely woman in Maynooth when the children were growing up. She wasn't married and had no children of her own, but she was determined that local children should have a place to play after school, that they should have somewhere to go at the weekend, and that they should learn some skills on top of what they learnt in the classroom. I remember watching her one St Patrick's Day in the parade in Maynooth.

She was walking along beside a big group of children, some of whom were in scout uniforms. I could see the love-of-life bursting from both her and the children. It was as if the whole group was bathed in a fine mist of love-of-life which was being lit up by little sparks of light. It was so beautiful to see. She looked quite severe, though, and only smiled occasionally. I was confused as her love-of-life was exploding from her and she should have been beaming. Her guardian angel told me that she didn't believe an adult should be too exuberant. She worked very hard to make these children happy, to connect them with love-of-life, but she held the view that adults shouldn't really be happy, and certainly shouldn't show it. I felt a little sad about this. Her devotion to the children has grown and nourished her love of life, but she was a little afraid to show just how happy she was.

God has told me that we are meant to be happy, that we are meant to love every step, every breath we take. Some people respond to this by saying, if this is true, 'Why doesn't God make it easier for us to love life?' I don't know why some people seem to have very tough lives, why they suffer ill health, or lose loved ones. I have no answer for this. I do think, though, that God has made it much easier to enjoy life than many people realise, and even when life is tough there is still so much to love.

We all have a responsibility to help each other to enjoy life through our actions (could your actions be having a *negative* impact on someone's enjoyment of life?), and through helping others to be aware of the joy that is in their lives. It's important that we reach out and try and help someone when that person has had a disappointment, a row, or feels down in some way. We are all connected, so it's important that we take responsibility for others who cross our paths, not just close friends or relatives. The angels tell me that if there was more of this reaching out, then fewer people would get to the point where they see taking their own life as the only way out.

The truth is that we all have the potential to reach this point of desperation, this point of darkness where your love-of-life is extinguished. If you think it could never happen to you or those you love, you are wrong, and one of the best ways to avoid ever reaching this point is to get into the habit of learning to love life, of seeing the good things that are there, even when things are very tough and challenging.

No one is supposed to end his or her own life. When people do, it's as if a link in a chain is broken and it slows down the progress of humanity. We all need one another. We are all connected because each and every one of us has a soul, and all of our souls are a part of God. Each and every one of us has a unique role to play in this world. No one else can play your part.

Each and every suicide in the world diminishes us. No matter if you don't know the person, their family, or even if they live on the other side of the world from you; their decision to end this life prematurely affects you. It silently shatters a part of you – even if you are not conscious of it.

When someone is thinking of ending his or her own life I see that person's guardian angel intertwined with them, as if trying to breathe a love-of-life back into them. The guardian angel, aided by other angels, will do its best to stop this person committing suicide. But these desperate people need our help too. We have an important role in helping to restore people's love-of-life, in helping to build up this energy and the vibrancy that will give them the positivity and courage to go on living.

Sometimes, even with all the help and love they are given by family and friends, by professionals and by the angels, the person may still feel unable to climb out of that darkness or to feel any spark of love-of-life. The pain is just too much for some – they cannot help themselves, and so go on to take their own lives.

As I say, no one is supposed to take his or her own life. If, however, someone does commit suicide, the angels have told me that they are wrapped in a blanket of God's love and are taken straight to heaven.

Many of us take so much for granted and it's often only when we have lost something that we really appreciate what we had. I was at the airport in Switzerland recently and was heading towards the loos when the angel with no name appeared behind me, just to my right. As I turned into a corridor, I saw a good-looking woman in her mid-thirties a little way ahead. She was in a wheelchair. The angel with no name told me that I was to offer to help her, but wasn't to go any closer. I was puzzled as to why I wasn't to go any closer, but asked her if I could help.

Her guardian angel opened up and on each side of the woman appeared large gold angels with wings. The angel on her right reached out and touched the woman's arm and she turned the wheelchair to face me.

I heard the angel with no name ask me, 'Can you see her love-of-life?' I couldn't have missed it; it burst out from her. Her guardian angel told me to ask again if I could help in any way. I did, and got a dazzling smile and head shake in response. Her love-of-life seemed to explode from her even more strongly. It was as if in my offering to help, and her affirming that she was committed to doing it on her own, she was releasing more love for life. It seemed to encircle her, coming from every part of her, energising her human body, giving it strength to live life to the full, even if it had limitations.

I watched the woman again. I could see her love for herself flowing from her and turning back like a wave to flow over her. She loved herself, and she loved life, and these two were feeding her, making her into a positive and happy woman who was able to take on the physical challenges she was facing with courage, strength and joy.

When we allow ourselves to love life, we release more of our self-love and grow in love.

CHAPTER TEN

Love of our planet

'WHAT'S THAT?' THE BOY OF ABOUT FIVE asked. He was pointing to a butterfly in a photograph of a beautiful meadow of flowers. There were a series of photographs and the children were questioning their teacher with wonder about all kinds of fantasy creatures like deer and birds, and amazingly beautiful flowers.

The children kept asking 'Why?' – as children do. 'Why didn't they take care of them for us?' 'Why did they allow this to happen?'

I watched as the class finished and the children went off to play. One little girl ran around with her hand in the air, imagining she was running after a butterfly that perched there, while two other children played at picking flowers.

The angels were showing me a future where we had neglected and destroyed much of our planet. I was so full of shame and sadness watching this vision, knowing that I was being shown something that could come to pass unless we all stop taking our planet for granted and allowing ourselves and others to destroy it.

I feel very upset while writing this chapter. God has given the earth an angel which is its protector, its gatekeeper. God gave us this angel so our planet could flourish and give us a glimpse of heaven. But this angel, Jimazen, like any angel, cannot overstep the boundaries of human will. If we refuse to listen and see the signs he is giving us, he is powerless to stop us.

If we continue to treat the planet the way we are, it will become barren and incapable of sustaining human life. Jimazen is giving us signs left, right and centre, but so many people are ignoring these signs – thinking that if it hasn't affected them personally, they don't need to worry about it. Natural disasters, changes in weather patterns, the black rhino becoming extinct, may not have personally affected you yet – but have no doubt if we don't wake up very soon, in the future you and your family will feel the impact of these signs.

I remember as a ten-year-old paddling in the sea on the east coast of Ireland. I was playing on my own, as I often did when I was a child. I was enjoying the feeling of the water around my ankles when I felt the sand tremble under my feet and saw these large circular ripples like waves forming. I saw first the staff he always holds, and then Jimazen was there. Jimazen is an enormous angel, like a giant. He was dressed in gold and red protective armour with a tinge of black. He looked down at me with love, but as always when I see Jimazen I could feel his anger and his frustration at how people were treating the planet.

On this particular day, some fifty years ago, he told me that we were destroying the sea with pollution. I didn't understand the word, so he explained to me: 'Man is putting loads and loads of dirt and bad things into the sea. People think it's a bottomless pit and anything can be put into it without affecting them, but they are so wrong. They have already killed off lots of life forms within the sea, and they will never get them back. Look down! This is what they have done.'

I looked down at what had been lovely clear seawater lapping around my ankles, and found that instead I was standing in a thick liquid, the consistency of custard, that was a disgusting black-green colour. I wriggled my toes, feeling very uncomfortable to be standing in this horrible liquid.

'That's what humans are doing!' Jimazen continued, full of frustration and anger. 'How can life exist in that?' With that, Jimazen disappeared. When I looked back down, it was lovely clear seawater I was standing in, but it didn't feel so good any more.

We all need to wake up and be more aware of the beauty and the gifts of nature that surround us. If we do not appreciate and love nature's incredible beauty, there is no way we will be prepared to do what is required to protect it.

A lot of people think protecting the environment has nothing to do with them. They believe that it's something for governments or activists. One of the things that Jimazen has asked me to tell you is that the more we hurt nature, the more we will hurt ourselves. The angels have told me to tell you that it's not just polar bears and animals that we might regard as exotic, and not a part of our daily lives, that will be affected by our abuse of this planet, but also our very means of survival. Jimazen has told me that the foot and mouth outbreak that occurred in Europe some years ago was caused by man, and was an example of what could happen if we don't care for our planet. Imagine a world where we have no livestock to feed ourselves, no meat, milk or eggs.

If we don't act it will be our grandchildren,

or their children, asking of us, 'How could they have done that? How could they have let it happen?'

We hold the future of this planet in our hands. This earth is a gift from God and has been given to each and every one of us for use in our lifetime. It doesn't belong to oil companies, multinationals, or governments. It belongs to us. We have been given this planet to live in, love and enjoy for our lifetime, but we have also been given the sacred task of passing it on to future generations.

 We all need to wake up and be more aware of the beauty and the gifts of nature that surround us.

Far too many decisions that affect our environment are tainted by greed and lobbying of special interests. We are all required to stand up and to make sure our leaders at neighbourhood, community, regional, national and international level know we care about this planet and our environment, and will hold them accountable. Already some of the damage is irreversible so there is no time to waste. All the money in the world will not be able to restore our planet if we continue as we are. Money is not going to be able to replace species of plants and animals, to clean our waters, to make our air healthy enough to breathe.

We mustn't forget either to pray for our planet, to pray that our leaders will listen and do the right thing, that multinationals will stop looking for unfair profit and start to look for ways of doing things that will benefit all; that the scientists, engineers and environmentalists will listen and make the breakthroughs they need to develop alternative cleaner ways of doing things.

The hole in the ozone layer is there whether people wish to believe it or not and it is growing because we keep pumping pollution into the environment. The angels have shown me the hole in the ozone layer. It was about fifteen years ago; I was sitting in the sunshine on the grass by the canal when I felt an angel touch my shoulder. I saw Angel Jimazen's staff, but I didn't see him, and then I found myself surrounded by a very fine mist. It was a beautiful blue, and crystal clear. I looked up, and above me I was shown what the angel behind me said was the hole in the ozone layer. I have no idea how I was allowed to see it.

I suppose I had always imagined the hole in the ozone layer to be round, but in reality it was very large and long. Then I was shown the edges of the hole in detail, as if with a zoom lens. The edges were very uneven and seemed to be rolling and smouldering, as if they were on fire – and yet I could see no flame. The edges were slowly being eroded and the hole was getting bigger.

I heard the angel tell me that this hole had been caused by Man. It explained that the fine blue mist surrounding me was being created by the planet in an effort to heal itself, but that the damage was too great and the planet couldn't heal itself on its own. I was also told that if the damage had come from outside of our world, Jimazen might have been able to act to protect it, but because humankind had caused this damage of its own free will, Jimazen is not able to act.

I was told that we had the ability to stop the growth of the hole in the ozone layer and repair the damage if we wished to. I don't know how we will repair the hole, but I am told that it will require all sorts of professions – scientists, engineers, environmentalists, computer scientists – to work together for our common good. It will not be solved if people are just out for themselves or wish to make unjust profit out of the process.

I know some people will be distressed to hear that I am told that the world's government's and institutions need to give mending the ozone layer a higher priority than economic recovery, or even disease or combating poverty, but if we don't solve this problem, it will make all these other challenges significantly worse.

We have to stop pumping chemicals into the atmosphere. I am also horrified at the growth in the process of gas extraction known as fracking. Angel Hosus has told me that it may create short-term jobs, but it is at the price of signing some people's death warrants. The angels tell me that fracking has to stop. We are poisoning our earth and feeding the hole in the ozone layer. No government should be sanctioning any company to frack, and people must stand up and say no to it happening anywhere in the world.

People worry about what will happen when we have used up all the oil on earth. The angels tell me, though, that if we take all the oil out of the earth it will have disastrous consequences for our planet. Man doesn't understand the role of oil in the earth, just as in previous times we didn't understand that the world was round. But I am being told that oil, like water, has a crucial role to play and that if we are greedy and strip the earth of all the oil that lubricates it, it will have catastrophic effects in terms of the stability of the earth, causing earthquakes, and even more upheaval in terms of weather patterns.

I was walking in a small forest in Ireland a few weeks ago. As I walked I became aware that there was a long line of angels following me. I wondered what they were up to, but didn't take too much notice as I was looking at the trees and listening to the birds. I stopped in a small clearing to watch a family of wrens who were nesting in a bush under the trees. There were four baby birds who were learning to fly. One of the parent birds kept flying from one branch to another, and waited while the babies caught up with him, practising their flying. They were chirping away as they did this.

In front of me was a big area of trees with two paths, one to the left and one to the right. I was told by the angels with me to stay where I was. The line of angels who had been behind me walked past me and down the path to the right, a path that then seemed to encircle the trees. There were hundreds of angels in a line and it took some minutes for them to pass. A few minutes later I saw some of the angels walking towards me from the left. I now saw that these angels had formed a huge circle surrounding the trees. The angels were standing looking at the trees and their arms were stretched out, fingertips touching.

Suddenly in one of the trees I saw the tree angel. As when I have seen her previously, the tree angel seemed to fill every part of the tree and move with every branch and leaf. I'm never sure whether the tree angel is moving with the tree, or the tree is moving with the angel. What really struck me about the tree angel, on this occasion, was just how sad she looked. If she had been human she would have been weeping.

The angels with me told me again to stay there, and not to move.

I saw the staff first, and knew Jimazen was coming. I saw Jimazen briefly and then it was as if he touched all the trees and there was a big flash of light, an explosion, and all the trees were gone. Where there had been hundreds of mature trees a moment before was now barren and desolate; all life was gone from this big area in front of me.

I was horrified. Now I knew why the tree angel was so devastated. I was being shown what could happen, how things would look, if we didn't care for our environment.

It stayed this way for about a minute, and I

looked at it in terror. Beside me the wrens sang, and I was conscious that if something like this happened to our planet, it wouldn't affect just our trees, but would affect so much of nature – there would be nowhere for the wrens and other birds and animals to live.

I have been told by the angels that we need to plant many more trees – that we need to plant millions and millions of them, that they should be broadleaf trees and that they should be planted as a long-term contribution to our future environment.

I know this is very daunting, and it's easy to get depressed or discouraged at how much we need to do. I see so much to be hopeful about, though. I have been shown visions of what our earth can be like if we do make the right decisions and take the steps. The angels have shown me a future where the earth is so green, so bright and so vibrant. When I saw it I realised just how much pollution has dulled the world in which we live now. In this future, the flowers were so colourful, rivers were crystal clear, and the sky was such a beautiful blue. I was allowed to feel the purity of the air I was breathing. It felt fresh and energised me.

The world looked so clean and so new. I know I wouldn't have been shown this if it weren't a realistic possibility, one that is within our grasp.

CHAPTER ELEVEN

Our unrealistic expectations of romantic love

ANGELS OF ROMANTIC LOVE LOOK DIFFERENT to other angels. They are tall and slender and are always dressed from head to toe in a very light cloak made of a fine fabric with tiny little square shapes, like a check of gold and a pastel amber, and I see the light of these beautiful angels radiating through these tiny little squares.

I recognise an angel of romantic love not just by the cloak, but also by a golden thread, full of light, that is attached somewhere to their clothing. It could be dangling from the shoulder or the waist or from the sleeve of the clothing. I've even seen the golden thread dangling just above where I sometimes see their bare toes.

This golden thread is a part of the angel of romantic love. It is connected to them and they use this thread to help to bind together a couple, and to feel more of each other's love. When the angels use this thread it encourages the couple involved to show their love more.

Romantic love is the only form of love that has its own type of angel to help. The angels tell me that this is because romantic love is meant mainly to help us to form families that can nourish and bring up happy children who are full of self-love and able to love others, people who are capable of imagining and creating a better future for our world.

Our children, and their children in turn, hold the future of our world in their hands.

Romantic love is very challenging for most people, because it requires us to put another person's needs on the same level as our own.

It's not, contrary to popular opinion, all sweetness and light. As well as a source of massive happiness and joy, it's a challenge and hard work.

One of the biggest barriers in romantic love is that so many people don't love themselves enough. I repeat – *if you don't love yourself, you are not able to love another fully*. So many people are looking to a romantic partner to complete themselves; but we are complete. We are all the same pure love we were as a baby, but the problem is we have locked away so much of it inside of us. We feel this absence of self-love in our lives but instead of unlocking it – and only we can do this – we seek someone special to love us to compensate for our lack of self-love.

I remember last summer watching an elderly man, who was enjoying a cup of tea in the sunshine outside Kilkenny Castle. The man was closely watching a couple in their late thirties who were sitting nearby holding hands and sharing an ice cream cone. The man's guardian angel opened up and it was bent over him embracing him, showering him with love and comforting him. The angel's wings were wrapped around him, and the tips of the wings seemed to touch the man's hands which were curled around the cup of tea he was drinking. He looked so sad. I couldn't see any self-love coming from him.

> **One of the biggest barriers in romantic love is that so many people don't love themselves enough.**

Angel Hosus was with me and told me that this man had very little self-love and that he was jealous of the couple's love. All of his life he had been in search of love, but he believed he had never found it. Angel Hosus continued, 'It was there but he missed it!'

The problem was that this man believed that the only love was romantic love, and as a result he'd missed out on all the opportunities for love that were around him; he missed out on the love of family and friends because he didn't give it any value. He still felt that way.

Hosus told me that this man had gone out with lots of women, but believed that none of them were the right one. He had failed to realise, as so many people have in the process of learning to love themselves, that they are not perfect. He thought he was perfect and the woman he fell in love with would be perfect, and that their life together would be perfect. He believed, as many do, in the promises of fairy tales and love songs. He had expectations of romantic love that no relationship could live up to and so he was left alone, without the love of family or friends, or that of a partner. As I got up to leave, his guardian angel leaned over and whispered something to the man and he looked over at me. I smiled at him. He didn't smile back. There was no love of himself there, no love of life and no happiness – and he was unable to see or respond to the smile of love from a stranger.

I was told that the angels of romantic love

were with him at different times in his life, trying to get him to be more realistic and to open himself more to love, and to give himself and the girl an opportunity of happiness. There was romantic love there for him, but he let it pass him by.

The angels of romantic love are there to assist us when we need help in romantic relationships. I have never seen them with anyone for any other reason.

Two years ago I was in the café of a garden centre near my home. As I paid for my coffee at the self-service counter I noticed an angel of romantic love standing beside a man in his forties who was sitting alone drinking a coffee.

After I had been sitting there a little while, the man came over and introduced himself. He told me that he recognised me from a television appearance a short time before. He sat down and we chatted for a few minutes. With embarrassment, he told me that he had never been out with a woman. I looked at him in surprise and asked him why not. He told me that he was shy and never knew what to say. I knew that the angel of love was there to help give him the courage to approach someone. I told him that the angels would help him, but that he himself was going to have to take his courage in his hands and ask a woman out – that much as the angels of romantic love might want to help him, they couldn't do that for him.

He left with a spring in his step, feeling he had some support to help him.

I was thrilled to meet him again over a year later, with a young woman he introduced to me as Jennifer. With them were two angels of romantic love and there was a golden thread tied around both of them at waist level. As we all three talked, the angels smiled at me, and pulled the thread a little tighter. He told me that not only had he got up the courage to ask her out, but he had also, after some months, asked her to marry him and they were getting married the following summer. Please God I'll meet them again sometime soon with a child in a pram.

I have a Canadian friend called Patrick, and

recently he brought his partner Richard over to Ireland to meet me. It was lovely to see the angels of romantic love with the two men as they strolled towards me holding hands. The angels were trying to get them both to be more aware and more considerate of each other's needs, and ensure that they were both happy and fulfilled by the decisions they were reaching. Even when talking about something relatively trivial like what to do the next day, I could see the angels of love whispering in each of their ears so that they would consider the other's wishes. This of course is something that all couples need to be aware of; and if I'm honest, I thought this couple were more considerate of each other's needs than many other couples I have met.

I meet many gay people, particularly young men who feel isolated and lonely because they fear it is unacceptable to be gay. I always tell them that God gave them, like everyone, a soul and a guardian angel and that God and their guardian angel knew before they were born whether they would be gay or straight. I see angels of romantic love helping same-sex couples and I know that they can also make excellent parents.

Sometimes people confuse lust with love. They are certainly not the same thing. I asked the angels how to talk about this and they told me to describe lust as being like an itch, a craving that gives temporary pleasure but that is insubstantial. Making love is a joy, a wonderful God-given gift which is an act of love, not just a source of physical pleasure. Indiscriminate sex is demeaning to all involved. We are spiritual as well as physical beings, even if we often forget this. Our soul is linked with our body. When we abuse our human body through indiscriminate sex, excessive use of alcohol or drugs, we debase our souls.

There is a disconnection between love and sexual activity in modern society and this is one of the reasons for the increase in prostitution. The angels have shown me how immoral it is for a person to use another human being in this way, and how degrading it is for all involved.

Romantic love is there to help to make it easier for us to have a loving and lasting relationship in which to bring up children. Not everyone can have children of their own blood. But many can adopt, foster or just be there for children. I keep repeating how important parenting or supporting children and young people is. They are our futures, the future of humanity.

I was asked to meet a couple in need of help. They arrived to meet me in a local café. The first thing I noticed was that there were two angels of romantic love with them, and that the angels had two golden threads tied around them at waist level. It's really unusual for me to see more than one thread around a couple, so I knew something was seriously wrong. They sat down and the husband started to talk. He told me that they had been married five years and that he loved his wife very much. As he said this, he reached out to touch her hand and I heard her say under her breath that she loved him too. She turned and looked at me with tears in her eyes and told me that he was physically unable to have children, and she felt she needed to leave him and find a man with whom she could have children.

'What about adoption?' I asked her. She rejected the idea out of hand. 'I want to have my own baby.'

We talked some more. I felt so sad for them; she was so sure that she needed to leave the marriage and he was unable to stop her, despite his protestation that he would never stop loving her.

As they walked away, one of the angels of romantic love took a thread away, although the other remained. I asked the angel why. 'She is so determined,' it said. 'We can't interfere with her free will, and if she refuses to listen to the suggestions we make there is little we can do. The sad thing is,' the angel continued, 'she does love him, and if they tried to adopt there is a good chance they would be successful and form a happy and loving family.'

Sustaining a loving marriage is hard work. We are living in a society that has created expectations that romantic love should be sweetness and happiness all the time – and when it isn't, couples often decide they want out of the marriage. Lots of couples break up where I am being told by the angels they shouldn't.

Couples have to work all the time to remind themselves why they fell in love in the first place, and to look back and reconnect with this love. With the pressures of modern life, marriage often becomes a chore and love is pushed to one side, with couples taking each other for granted. Both parties need to make an effort to keep this love alive. This is one of the things I frequently see angels of romantic love doing – encouraging couples to show each other love. I often see them encouraging people to make small gestures, or take ten minutes in an otherwise busy day to sit and chat with each other.

There is a couple I have met several times over the past five years. When I met them first they had been married three years and had a young son of one and a half. The young man told me that he wanted out of the marriage; that he was deeply unhappy. I asked him what relationship he had with his little son. He told me he had none! As he said this, I saw him pull his self-love in even tighter, shutting even more of it away. One of the angels of romantic love with them told me that he didn't even want to hold the child, so that it wouldn't hurt him as much when he left.

The young man told me that his wife hadn't gone back to work since the child was born and that he hadn't bargained on having to look after everyone financially. He also told me that he hadn't expected to lose his freedom, and that he deeply resented it when he had to put her, or his son's needs, before his own.

He told me he didn't love his wife, although the angels of romantic love told me this wasn't true. The angels of romantic love were working hard to keep this couple together, but they kept telling me that this young man had an awful lot of growing up to do. They told me he was hiding the love he was feeling because he felt overwhelmed by the responsibility.

These angels also told me to encourage him to stay, at least for a while, and to coax him to get to know his son more – to pick him up and hold him, and let the love be stirred up within him.

I have met this couple over the years, and sometimes it looked as if they would make it as a family, and sometimes they would be yet again on the verge of splitting. But with the help of the angels of romantic love, and the support of others – including me – they have stayed together. I know they are meant to stay together and hope that with the help of the angels the young man will learn to see the love and joy within his family rather than only the responsibilities. If we are prepared to really try to save a relationship, the angels of romantic love and other angels will give us tremendous support.

Sometimes in a marriage love is pushed aside and bitterness and hate creep in. Bitterness and hate are like cancers that eat away at love. When this happens between a couple, I will see what looks like a thin but strong dark shield covering their hearts, protecting them from feeling any love or compassion. It is so horrible to see. A couple become so cold-hearted and start to want revenge. Revenge is an insidious desire and it can colour how people behave for years and years, making them continually try to point score and get back at each other – frequently using their children as ammunition.

We all have the free choice to stop this bitterness and hate creeping in. We do it by making a conscious decision to stop when we feel provoked, to consciously choose not to react. We have to make this choice over and over again, and try to be calm for an hour, or for a day.

Many marriages and relationships break up that shouldn't do, and it would be better for all involved if the couple persevered, stuck together, and learnt to love each other again. At times, though, I have been shown that a couple needs to split up, particularly if there has been physical or mental abuse. In these cases, the children will be better off with the parents apart.

Parents need to be aware of the high cost their children have to pay when parents split up. The angels have told me that the break-up of the parents' marriage may reduce the chances of their children trusting sufficiently to have a loving and steady relationship as adults. It can make the child feel unloved and takes away its self-confidence. Some children believe that they are to blame for their parents' marriage break-up.

I remember a young woman in her late twenties called Olivia who came to talk to me. She told me she had gone out with a few men, but that she felt no man could really be trusted.

As she said this, the angel with no name appeared beside me and whispered into my ear that I was to ask her why she felt this. I did.

'My father walked out on my mum when I was ten,' she replied. 'They were always arguing and fighting and I was very scared all the time.' Tears welled up in her eyes. 'I thought it was my fault, that I had done something wrong, and that if I was good they wouldn't be fighting all the time.' She told me that she had never ever seen her dad since he left, and that she still felt it was her fault that he had gone. She also blamed him for abandoning her and for not keeping in contact with her.

She told me her mother never talked about her father. When I suggested that she should talk to her mother about him, she shook her head. 'Mum was so angry for years after he left. She still is really. She cried so much and was mad at me and everyone who came into the house. I couldn't bring up all that again. It wouldn't be fair to Mum.'

The angel with no name whispered in my ear to ask her another question. I did: 'When you go home, ask your mother whether your father ever sent you a birthday card?'

She looked at me strangely as if it was an odd question. I told her to ask gently, and not to fight or get angry with her mother, but that she needed to get an answer to this question.

Three months later Olivia rang me and asked whether we could meet again. She told me that each time she started asking her mother about her father, her mother would react with anger, saying she hated Olivia's father. Eventually, though, Olivia got from her mother the admission that each year her father had sent Olivia a birthday card and that each year she had torn it up. She was so caught up with her desire for revenge that she never seemed to have thought about the impact her behaviour was having on her daughter.

Olivia hadn't reacted with anger or judgement of her mother. She asked her mother whether it was her fault that they had split up. 'How could you have ever thought that – you were just a child?' her mother replied in horror. She had been so caught up in her own pain that she had never thought there was any need to reassure her little daughter.

Eventually Olivia got her mother to admit that while she had no contact with her father, her sister, Olivia's aunt, did. For the first time since he had left when she was ten, Olivia got to meet her father. She discovered that far from abandoning her, he used to come and watch her walking home from school, staying far enough away that she wouldn't see him. Olivia's mother would allow him no access, and to keep the peace he stayed away, but he always kept in contact with Olivia's aunt so he could find out how she was.

Olivia said that perhaps now she was ready to start trusting men. The angel with no name told me that it would be very hard for her, though, to overcome all those years of believing that a man had abandoned her; even though she now knew that it was not true.

I asked the angel with no name if Olivia's parents could have patched things up and I was told yes, but that they allowed bitterness and hate to take them over. As I gave Olivia a goodbye hug, I thought of how different life would have been for her if her parents had worked on their relationship and stayed together.

Sometimes a marriage just doesn't work, and in the end both sides need to accept that pain and hurt and start to live life again. They shouldn't give up on life – or love – and need to be open to allowing romantic love back into their life again.

If romantic love is in your life already, do everything you can to cherish it and to keep the relationship blossoming. If it's not in your life at this moment, be open to it, and be realistic in your expectations. Give yourself and the other person the chance of the joy that comes with romantic love.

CHAPTER TWELVE

Loving your enemies and those you find hard to love

EACH AND EVERY ONE OF US IS UNIQUE AND perfect. We all have a unique role to play in this world, a role that no one else can play. And yet we waste so much of our lives comparing ourselves to others. This might seem harmless, but it's one of the seeds of hate.

Hatred can creep so easily into our lives if we are not conscious of it. We all need to become conscious of the times we are tempted to give in to hate, even in what seem like small ways. We need to lose the automatic instinct to strike back. No matter how much you have been hurt, the angels tell me that giving into feelings of hatred and seeking revenge is always the wrong thing to do.

We all have to work to overcome hate in our own lives. It's a matter of free will. No one can make us love and no one can make us hate; we have free choice, and we need to be more conscious of the choices we are making. Hatred and revenge keep us going around in negative circles and there is only one way to break this cycle: this is by becoming aware of our hate, saying no to it, and choosing instead to show some compassion – both to others involved and ourselves.

Recently I was sitting in a café and at a table near me was a group of six students. The table was surrounded by angels and the angels told me to listen to what was being said. They started talking about a girl who wasn't there, a girl called Gloria, a Nigerian. They called her all kind of names and ran her down in a very nasty and spiteful way. The angels told me that one of the reasons for this was that Gloria was very intelligent and attractive. The other was that they disliked her because she was different, a dislike based on ignorance. The angels keep telling me how important it is to treat people, or groups of people, we don't understand with compassion and love. We are far too quick to judge. These young people didn't want to allow in any understanding of the girl and her life and where she came from. They weren't willing to learn, and were failing to take advantage of the opportunities that being in a college with people of different nationalities was giving them. This incident was about nationality, or perhaps colour, but it could as easily have been about religion, sexual orientation, political belief or any of the myriad of things that we choose to judge people on.

The guardian angel behind one of the girls opened up. It was massive, towering over her and dressed in blue with light coming through. It had its arms encircling her as if giving her strength, and it looked down at her with great love and compassion – but also with concern. It looked up at me and asked me to say a prayer that the girl he was guarding would listen to him and would have the courage to do what she needed to do.

Suddenly one of the boys turned on the girl whose guardian angel had opened up, saying, 'You know her, I've seen you with her. How could you spend any time with a . . .' The abuse about Gloria continued and the girl at the table started silently crying – she didn't say anything though. The angels were moving around the table at speed, trying to get these young people to put love and compassion into their hearts, to help them to see that tearing this girl apart was wrong.

No matter what the angels did, the others didn't listen. They continued giving out about Gloria. They were very negative and very hard and were feeding off one another. When one would say something negative, another would add something else. They were self-satisfied and sure of themselves. They were caught up in their rant.

Hatred feeds on itself so much more easily than love. It can build and spread very fast, building up a cycle of hatred. When hatred is allowed to build up, it also becomes very difficult for love and compassion to penetrate it. When we allow hatred into our hearts it displaces love, and makes us lock more of it away.

Shortly after, four of them left, leaving the girl and one of the boys there. The angels all stayed with the pair remaining at the table. I briefly wondered why. The remaining boy looked over at the girl and said, 'How well do you know her anyway?' I think he expected her to say 'hardly at all'.

She looked up at him and I remember the way her guardian angel straightened up and put its hands on her shoulders. The girl straightened up too and gave the young man a look of deep sadness, and said bitterly, 'Gloria is my best friend and I have just let her down.'

The young man's face fell. It was as if he suddenly realised what he had been a part of. It was as if he suddenly heard all the messages that the angels had been trying to get him to hear while the conversation was going on. He sat there in silence, deeply ashamed of himself.

The girl sat there for a few minutes with him. She too was devastated – both by the behaviour of her group of friends and by her own failure to stand up for Gloria. Her guardian angel looked over at me and told me that it had been trying to get her to have the courage to speak up and defend her friend. The angel also told me that if she had spoken up earlier on she would have stopped the conversation; that they would not have built up their hatred in the way that they did.

We all need to be aware when hurtful or hateful things are being said about people. We all have a responsibility to stop cycles of hatred being built up. This applies to each one of us as individuals in relation to gossip, or talking negatively about people. In recent times our media have too often fanned the flames of hatred, sowing divisions between different groups. The media are extremely important and have a crucial part to play in building a better world, but far too often they build division, jealousies and hatred – going for the sensational rather than seeking to expose the truth.

Jealousy can also be a seed of hate and can destroy a lot of the joy in a life. There was a man I used to bump into occasionally who lived in a large house near me in Maynooth. He had lots of money and a beautiful home, but each time I met him he would always bring up his cousin who had inherited a small business from their uncle. He believed that the business should have been left to him and implied that his cousin had obtained the business under false pretences. He seemed completely unable to even consider the possibility that his uncle had left the business to his cousin and not to him because he already had plenty of money and his cousin had very little. He continually ran down his cousin and his family, calling them wasters. He said they were no good, and that he hoped the business would go bust.

Each time I saw him I saw his guardian angel open up. This angel had huge love and compassion for him, and was constantly trying to get him to soften his heart and to let go of the jealousy and bitterness. He wouldn't listen, though; he was eaten away by the jealousy. It was a complete obsession with him and he seemed unable to talk about anything else. Sometimes I would see his guardian angel making a gesture with its hands, trying to get him to move on: but to no avail.

I've met so many people over the years who have been eaten away by jealousy of someone else. Often the other person is either not aware of the jealousy or not concerned by it and is simply getting on with making his or her own life, while the jealous person is paralysed by hate. Sometimes years later the jealous person wakes up, and realises that life has passed them by while he or she was busy being preoccupied by jealousy and resentment.

Jealousy doesn't just happen between people; it happens between organisations, religions, countries. Even organisations that are set up to help people at times allow jealousy in; I recently came across a charity jealous that people were giving more money to another charity than to them!

I'm not talking about competition. Competition and jealousy are completely different forces. Competition helps people to be more creative, to be more open, to strive to find new ways of doing things and making things better. Competition helps build things up, often making things better for many. Jealousy is about pulling someone or something down. Competition spurs us on to greater things, but jealousy diminishes us and others.

Our world would be a much better place to live in if there were less jealousy and envy among our leaders and institutions. Jealousy (or fear) that another country, political party or institution might do better than us blocks people in power from seeing solutions to problems – solutions that would benefit us all.

Become conscious of not allowing hate to creep into your life. It can happen so easily. Someone can have an argument with his or her boss over something trivial – like wanting time off that the boss won't give. Feeling angry and hard done by, the person starts to think of all the negative things his or her boss has ever done (never the positive things) and hate creeps in and grows. We all need to be continually vigilant about not allowing hate in.

Anger is one of the ways that we feed hate. It's a habit for many people, a bad one, and can become a way of life. I remember a farmer I met in my late teens, when I was out fishing with my father. I have rarely met anyone who was as angry as this man was. He was angry at everyone and everything; no one could do anything right. He was even angry at the grass as it wouldn't grow the way he wanted it to.

He believed he was right and everyone else was wrong, and he used this as an excuse as to why nothing ever turned out right in his life. His farm was in a terrible state and, as far as he was concerned, it was all other people's fault.

It was really sad to see how his anger permeated the entire family and farm. His wife was full of negativity and fear. I watched her angrily shove a chair that was in her way. It was an unnecessary gesture, and when I asked the angels why she had done it, they told me that she had picked up from him the habit of being constantly angry at everything around her. It had become a way of life, a way of life they both passed on to their children. Their children, particularly their eldest son, knew of nothing else but to be angry and to blame the world.

I used to think of that family often and say a prayer that some of the children would break out of the cycle of anger and hate. I never saw the family again, but my father did occasionally, and I did once ask him – some ten years after I had originally met them – whether there had been any change. At that point, he said there hadn't.

Anger takes the joy and pleasure out of life, and it is a habit that is easy to get into. People who are angry are looking all the time for someone they can blame, an excuse for why things aren't going well for them in their lives. Ironically some of the people who are most angry have quite a lot in life, but they don't see this. The fire of anger burning inside of them is fed by little slights; very small things can become big issues for them – someone not answering a phone, someone ignoring them, a story in a newspaper. In feeding this flame of anger inside them they allow it to consume them, and this locks away more love.

 Hate gets into our hearts through jealousy, bitterness and anger and it takes on a life of its own.

There is a different sort of anger that is directed at injustices in the world, an anger that champions and helps to lead to positive change. If we examine our feelings deeply and honestly, we will recognise the difference between anger tainted with hate and righteous anger that is intertwined with compassion and love.

Righteous anger gives you the courage to stand up for yourself and, if necessary, to take the steps to protect yourself, those you love, and the things you believe are right. The angels are telling me that there is more righteous anger coming forward in the world now; that people are calling out for institutions and leaders to be made accountable. This increased demand for transparency may make it look at present as if the world is crumbling, but I am continually being assured by the angels that this is a step for the good. That people and organisations being held accountable is a necessary stage on the way towards a brighter future.

Unfortunately, though, righteous anger can turn into hateful anger, and people who take on a justifiable cause need to keep reminding themselves of the reasons why they had righteous anger within them. This way, they don't lose connection with the source of the righteous anger. They have to keep looking to the original focus – the injustice, the wrongdoing, the love and compassion for others – that ignited that righteous anger in the first place. Far too often what starts off as righteous anger to address some injustice gets out of control, spiralling into an anger that is full of hate and a desire for revenge. The angels, though, tell me that with awareness and continual questioning, righteous anger can be kept pure, untainted by hate, and that then it is a major force for good in our world.

Sadly, righteous anger that has become tainted by hate and revenge is a major cause of war and violence in our world.

Last year I flew to Zagreb to do a book tour. When we were in the airport in Dublin the angels brought my attention to a group of eight men aged from their late twenties to early fifties drinking in the bar. The airport was quite crowded and I didn't take much notice of them. As I boarded the plane and walked to my seat at the back, I saw the same group of men, surrounded by angels. The light of the guardian angel behind one of the men opened up. This angel towered over him and seemed to have its arms wrapped around the man with great love and compassion. It spoke to me without words, telling me to keep my head down and not to look at the men, not to attract their attention.

I didn't understand, but I did exactly as the

angel told me. I took my seat. Beside me in the window seat was a young man who was surrounded by tall slender angels.

It was hard to avoid looking at the group of men who were seated a few rows ahead of me on the other side. They were very loud, and talking in drunken voices in a language I couldn't understand.

Some while into the flight, the angels with the young man in the window seat told me I should start a conversation with him. We talked about where he was going and the work he did. It wasn't an easy chat as he seemed irritated and annoyed. The angels assured me I wasn't the cause of this, and told me to keep talking. I asked him if he was nervous of flying. As I did, an angel told me to glance at the group of men. I did, and at that moment the light of guardian angels behind all of the men opened up.

I turned back briefly to the young man and his guardian angel opened up too. This guardian angel gave a male appearance and held a long and slender handful of light in front of the young man at chest level as if to caress his heart. I could see a beautiful light coming from the guardian angel's hand. On his face was a look of enormous love and compassion.

The young man turned to me and started to talk in a low but firm voice. He clearly didn't want anyone to overhear what he was saying. 'Don't look over at those men! They are filth! Animals! If you could understand what they are saying, you would be horrified. My country was at war with them for a long time and they haven't changed. During the war they would creep into a village at night and kill everyone. They were such cowards that they murdered defenceless children. They had no mercy. My God, how I hate them.'

I looked down at the young man's hands and I could see his knuckles clenched tightly; they were as white as snow. His guardian angel then spoke to me without words, telling me that this young man was struggling with hate and a desire for revenge.

The young man told me horrific stories his grandfather had told him when he was a child. Horrendous stories about death, loss and destruction of property. He told me about things he himself had witnessed as a child. I could see the depth of the hatred and the desire for revenge within this young man.

His guardian angel told me to ask him whether he had any children. I did. He said no – he wasn't married, but that he hoped he would be one day.

I asked him how he would feel about his children growing up with such hatred and revenge in their hearts.

The young man looked at me for a few moments. 'How can you crush hatred and revenge? How can I do that when they are showing off at every opportunity they get? Sniggering and bragging in loud voices? You don't understand how obnoxious they are. I hate them. I would kill them all if I could.'

My heart went out to this young man. He was so eaten up with this hatred that he could see no way out of it. I told him what Angel Elijah had told me years before: 'War is easy to make, but peace is the hardest thing to keep.'

He looked at me as if this was a nice idea – but completely unrealistic.

We kept talking, though. We talked about the world he would like his children to grow up in, and he agreed he didn't want his children to grow up with war and violence around them. We talked about his hatred. When I mentioned forgiveness and the power that could come from it, he threw his eyes to heaven in exasperation. His guardian angel opened beside him and told me to keep talking – that I might think that I was wasting my breath, but that the message was getting through. Despite his best efforts, he was hearing what I was saying and he was starting to think about what a future without hatred would be like, for him and his children.

The conversation seemed to come to a natural end. The young man seemed to go deep into his thoughts. He stopped being bothered by the men; it was as if he didn't hear them anymore, although they were as loud as ever. I know what I had said gave him food for thought. He was full of hatred and anger. What had probably been righteous anger several generations before had become tainted with hatred, and this hatred was being fed by the harassment and provocation that he had felt on the plane. It is so hard for people to step out of the cycle of hatred, to decide that they won't seek revenge.

As he sat there lost in thought, I glanced over at the group of men again. I caught the eye of one of the younger men. Slightly to my surprise, I didn't see a look of defiance and anger there, but rather a look of shame, as if he felt I could see what he and his friends had been up to, and he was ashamed of being a part of this. His guardian angel opened up behind him again and this time it spoke to me. It told me that the loudest of the men was this boy's uncle and that he had brought him up – that this young man had grown up with his uncle telling him stories of hatred and boasting about the acts of revenge and aggression he had committed. His guardian angel asked me to pray that this young man would also break out of the cycle of violence and hatred.

I have been told by some people that they find this story depressing. But I see it as a story of hope, because what I was being shown was that these two young men were aware that they had the freedom to decide that they didn't want to continue this cycle, that they knew they had the potential to decide to break the cycle of hate and revenge within their own families, so that it wouldn't be passed on to their children in the way it had been passed on to them.

So often hate that is rooted in the past, even the distant past, is dragged into the future, cursing future generations. Many of us are lucky enough not to have grown up in places that are torn apart by war or violence, but many of us still carry hatreds that are rooted in the past; beliefs that others are inferior to us because of creed, education, class, colour, sexual orientation or nationality; sometimes it is even hatred within a family. We all need to be constantly vigilant as to when we may be keeping hateful attitudes from the past alive, and even passing them on to future generations.

I didn't get to have any further conversation

with the young man who had sat next to me, other than to say goodbye to him as I left the plane. He and the other young man are constantly in my prayers though. I pray they will have the courage and strength to break the cycle and to bring up their children free of the taint of hatred.

Hatred is such a negative emotion. Hate gets into our hearts through jealousy, bitterness and anger and it takes on a life of its own, feeding on everything negative that happens. People can go through their whole lives and still hate a person over something trivial that happened when they were children. We stop the cycle of hatred only by being conscious of hatred when it rises up in us, by starting to notice where it comes from, and what provokes it in us.

We all encounter adversity and challenges in our lives; we are all tempted to give in to hate, and most of us do occasionally, but we do always have a choice not to. When we choose not to give in to hate, not to feed it with negative thoughts, we allow our lives to be much more fulfilled. When we have hatred in our hearts we are not able to release the love that is there.

If we find we have given in to hate, we can still have self-compassion and forgive ourselves. When you try and root hatred out, when you look at yourself and those you hate with compassion, so much changes. You start to see the good in the person or people you hated, as well as the goodness and love within you.

Forgiveness has such enormous power; and if we realised the gift that comes from forgiving ourselves or from forgiving others, we would be much quicker to forgive. The key to forgiveness is looking at yourself and others with compassion and understanding. Let me describe what I see when someone says sorry to another, means it, and is forgiven. I saw this last week when my teenage daughter Megan apologised to a friend after a falling out.

As Megan said 'sorry', I saw a burst of the force of love come from both girls and flow over them as if showering them with love. It was a very high intensity of love in this moment, even though the girls were not particularly close friends. I saw each of their guardian angels move forward, bringing their arms around the girls as if encircling the two of them. The angels became brighter at this moment; to me it's as if they were celebrating and cementing the act of forgiveness. I was shown that in asking forgiveness and in forgiving, both girls had released more of the love they had locked away.

This happens each time someone says sorry and means it; each time someone forgives another.

When people forgive themselves, something similar happens. The force of love bursts forth from them and showers them, lighting them up. This light seems to go back into them, filling them with light and love. The guardian angel encircles them, as if giving them an enormous hug.

Forgiveness is such an enormous gift to us in helping to break the cycles of jealousy, anger or hate. It's such a shame that the angels tell me that many people are either too stubborn or too proud to accept this gift. When we forgive ourselves and others we crush hate, and this allows us to release love that is locked away within us, leaving us feeling happier and more able to see and appreciate the good things in our lives.

Love makes us better members of our families and society generally. Hate sows so many seeds of entitlement. People who have a lot of hate in them feel they are entitled, and can't see any reason to do something if there isn't something in it for them. There are so many things we can all do to make this world better for a neighbour, a stranger, our environment, for everyone. When people are consumed by anger, jealousy or hate, they lack love and fail to notice these opportunities and live a life that is much more limited.

Feelings of hate stop us, our families, our communities and our world from being happy and reaching our full life potential.

CHAPTER THIRTEEN

Love from Heaven

LONG, LONG AGO WHEN GOD CREATED THE
first few human beings, he fell in love with us,
and it was because of this that he decided he
would give all human beings a soul. Archangel
Michael told me this with a smile. He explained
that it was during the time that God was
creating life that he looked at what he was
making and fell in love with humans. He fell
in love with everything about us, including our
imperfection. He loved us in a way that was

different to any of his other creations. Because of this, he decided to give us something unique, something that would differentiate each and every human being from other life that he created.

God gave each and every one of us a part of himself, that speck of light of God that is our soul. We cannot comprehend how infinite God's love is, how pure and never-ending it is. In giving each of us a soul that is a speck of light of himself, God gave us a unique and powerful gift, the ability to love.

This is why I say love comes from heaven.

Angel Michael told me he was going to help me understand more about where love comes from. He took my soul, and suddenly I was in heaven and among a sea of souls, a soul for each and every member of the human race. I was told that all the souls that would ever be needed for all of humanity were there. I couldn't see where the souls began or ended.

I was just put in among them. The feeling was one of overwhelming love. I was in the presence of all these souls who were each individually a speck of the light of God and so I was in the presence of God.

The souls were waiting for God to appoint a guardian angel for each one of them. I watched a guardian angel walking among the sea of souls from some distance away. It was walking among millions of souls, but it knew where it was going. It walked directly towards the soul that it had been appointed gatekeeper of.

The guardian angel found the soul it had been appointed to guide and it was as if there was an explosion of love between the soul and the guardian angel as they encountered each other for the first time. The guardian angel and the soul embraced each other tightly; it was as if they stepped into each other.

I watched as this guardian angel and the soul walked towards God. It was as if it was a long, long journey and I was allowed to watch each step. During this time the soul and the guardian angel were talking to each other, sharing with great love and joy getting to know each other.

Finally, the soul and the guardian angel stood

in front of God. God embraced the soul and called it 'my child'.

Each of us is a child of God, we are pure love and we have the choice to let out more of the love that we have locked away.

Standing in front of God the real connection between the guardian angel and soul is made. Because of God's overwhelming love for us, his children, he has appointed a guardian angel as gatekeeper of our souls and has charged it with bringing us back safely home to him in heaven. God is waiting on each and every one of us to come home.

Your guardian angel can never leave you. It doesn't *want* to leave you anyway; it is constantly in the presence of your soul, which is a speck of the light of God, so that your guardian angel is continuously in God's presence. This is God's gift to your guardian angel – to allow it to stand for eternity in his presence.

As they stood there before God, the soul was allowed to choose its parents. It chose its parents (knowing all about them) and loved them unconditionally.

God spoke to the guardian angel, telling it to take this soul to be conceived in the human body of its chosen mother. The guardian angel was also reminded that this soul in its human body had been given the freedom to make decisions and choices and that the guardian angel was to respect this free will that human beings have been given and not to overstep the boundaries.

The guardian angel holds on to the soul with its hands and brings it from heaven to earth, just as it will do at the end of a life, bringing the soul back to heaven. At the moment of conception the guardian angel gently places the soul within the tiny human body and stays there within the womb, holding on to the soul until the moment of birth. The guardian angel is born with the baby, still holding on to its soul, but immediately after birth it lets go of the soul, allowing the human being to have freedom to make its own choices and make its own decisions.

Your guardian angel loves you unconditionally because you are pure love; no matter how much love you might lock away during your lifetime, your guardian angel always knows you as the pure love you were when it first met you in heaven.

Your guardian angel already knows that part of our human imperfection is that most of us will lock away a huge amount of our love – though it will do its best to stop you.

Your guardian angel is also always helping you to unlock the love that you have already locked away. Every time your guardian angel gets you to laugh or to enjoy something, it is helping you to unlock another bit of love, and it can help you to do this throughout your life.

Your guardian angel never gives up on you. It stood before God when God called you 'my child' and was appointed the gatekeeper of your soul. Your guardian angel is in constant contact with God about you. Humanly, this is very difficult for us to imagine, let alone understand that God cares about the joy and the happiness as well as the hurt and pain that you, and each one of us, feels while living a human life. God's love is so incredible, it is unfathomable.

I am told there will be some people reading this who will be asking 'Is this "my God" she is talking about? Is this the Christian, the Islamic, the Jewish God?' I could keep on listing different religions and faiths. So many people of different faiths want to believe that their God is superior to another religion's God, or that their God is the only real one.

God is God! There is only one God and we all share him. God stood before every one of our souls, before we were associated with any religion, and called each of us 'my child'. We are all God's children, regardless of where or how we pray, or whether we pray at all. I keep being told that the sooner we realise that all religions are one, and should be under the same umbrella, and the sooner we start to pray together, the better and more loving our world will be.

God loves us so much that he sent his son Jesus to live among us and experience life as a human.

I know I have said that we are all God's children, so I have asked the Archangel Michael how I can describe the difference between God's son Jesus and the rest of us. This is how he has told me to explain it. We are all God's children. We have each and every one of us been given a speck of the light of God, our soul. Jesus is much more than this. He is a much bigger part of God. Jesus can walk into God and become complete with him, whereas no *soul* can walk into God and become complete with him.

God loves us very much. Before he sent his son Jesus to live among us and to experience the joy and the pain of human life, he didn't fully understand us. He couldn't fully comprehend how we, who were made of pure love, could lock so much love away. How we, who were given a world full of beauty and abundance, could create and allow famine and war. I am told that for God to learn to understand us fully Jesus had to experience all the emotions that humans do – the joys and the pain. I am told that Jesus locked away love in his heart, to protect himself from hurt as we all do. God did not interfere or save him from those painful emotions. Jesus cried in the garden of Gethsemane the night before the crucifixion, wondering how his father in heaven could let this happen. Yet ultimately, through prayer, he got the strength and courage to unlock his love.

God needed Jesus to die in a heart-rending way to help to demonstrate to us just how great his love for us is; to give us a glimpse of this love that is incomprehensible to we humans. Jesus came to help everyone of all faiths and none; he was born into and practised the Jewish faith, yet he was here for all. He rose from the dead so that all humanity could live for ever.

Jesus took back to heaven all his experiences of living as a human, and now God understands us much better. He has more compassion and understanding for the things that make us strike out against others, and for how we lock away love and harden our hearts. This is why the God of the Old Testament is so different from the God of the New Testament.

God sees everything we do. We can't hide the smallest thing from him. When we do good things, are kind to ourselves or others, God smiles on us and that helps us to release more of the love we have locked away. I am told that when we do terrible things to each other, God cries. Yet if we say sorry and really mean it, he always forgives us.

Archangel Michael has told me of something beautiful that happens very occasionally. It occurs when everyone in the world shows love; it doesn't take major acts of love, it could just be to smile at a stranger, or wish someone well. What is important is that everyone in the world participates. When this happens, it's like a wave of love across the world, and in response to this human love God multiplies it, telling the guardian angels to help to release some extra of the love that is locked away within each and every person's heart.

Angel Michael tells me that the last time a

wave of love like this occurred was during the Second World War and that it had a major impact on humanity.

I don't know exactly when it happened; I have just been told it was during the Second World War. Humanly, I have always presumed that this was the beginning of the end of the war, but Angel Michael will not confirm this for me.

I don't know why it happened. It is tempting to say that this happened because mankind was facing an abyss and God intervened to stop us from completely destroying the world. But Angel Michael has told me this is not true, that God will not over-ride our free will – even when we are destroying ourselves.

It happened because each and every person in the world showed love or thought loving thoughts around the same time; perhaps it was brought about because of prayer, perhaps because people had had enough of war, perhaps because they listened to their guardian angels – whatever it was, they all performed acts of love and, in response, God told the guardian angels to help everyone to release more love into the world, multiplying the effect of the loving actions performed by each and every person.

I so wish that this would happen again soon. It could if each one of us realised that we are a child of God, that we are pure love, and that we have the *choice* to let out more of the love that we have locked away.

Appendix – Prayer of Thy Healing Angels

In *Angels in my Hair* I tell the story of the evening that Archangel Michael gave this prayer to me, and from that day on I have given it to people who come looking for help. All angels do healing work, but there is a particular group of angels called 'healing angels', which are called in by guardian angels when healing is required. There are literally millions of healing angels, and God is pouring healing angels on the world all the time. All we have to do is ask for their help.

We must always remember that the healing will happen in the way that God knows is best for us. Sometimes we may not recognise that healing has occurred, as it may not be the healing we have asked for – it may be emotional or spiritual healing rather than physical. We need to watch out for healing and recognise when it has been granted. Often healing can seem small: perhaps somebody who has been depressed for a long time smiles or laughs; maybe someone who was in a lot of physical distress feels a lot better; or maybe a mother who has been stressed out and unable to cope suddenly feels happiness and joy.

Many people have told me that the healing angels have helped in response to this prayer and over the years I have been told a lot of stories of people believing they, or those they loved, were helped by this prayer. Many people have told me they have written out the prayer to carry it around with them, or to give it to someone else.

Prayer of Thy Healing Angels,
That is carried from God by Michael, Thy Archangel.
Pour out, Thy Healing Angels,
Thy Heavenly Host upon me,
And upon those that I love,
Let me feel the beam of Thy
Healing Angels upon me,
The light of Your Healing Hands.
I will let Thy Healing begin,
Whatever way God grants it,
Amen.

To find out more about Lorna Byrne go to www.lornabyrne.com

Here you can:

- Add your wishes and prayers to Lorna's prayer scroll.

  'Years ago the angels handed me a prayer scroll and told me that when I was praying I should hold it in my hand and that the angels would join me in praying for everything contained within it.

  When I'm in a meditative state of prayer I hold in my hand this spiritual scroll with every name and every request written on it and I hand this scroll to God.

  I invite you to send me your thoughts, joys and worries so that they can be included.

  I won't be able to reply individually to your notes but be assured I will make sure they are included in the prayer scroll and in my and the angels' prayers. There is naturally no charge and everything is treated with confidence.'

  LORNA

- Sign up to receive Lorna's quarterly email newsletter.

- Read more of the wisdom that Lorna has been given by the angels.

- See where Lorna is speaking and doing signings.

- Watch videos and read interviews with Lorna.

Twitter: @lornabyrne
Facebook: Angels in My Hair by Lorna Byrne

ALSO BY LORNA BYRNE

A Message of Hope from the Angels

From the internationally bestselling author of *Angels in my Hair* comes The Sunday Times Number One bestseller with messages of hope for you.

In *A Message of Hope from the Angels* Irish mystic Lorna Byrne brings a vital, urgent communication from above for these challenging times.

'The Angel told me, "Hope makes the impossible possible."'

Lorna sees angels with as much clarity as the rest of us see people and she speaks to them every day. In the past Lorna has talked about her life, and how the angels prepared her to deliver a message to the world. This book contains her message of hope, and this message is for you.

She writes about how she sees angels helping people when they are feeling tired, helpless, depressed, unloved, inadequate as a parent, struggling financially or simply too busy.

In *A Message of Hope from the Angels* Lorna tells in a simple and direct way how you can call on this help to make your life better and happier.

CORONET

ALSO BY LORNA BYRNE

Stairways to Heaven

The overwhelming response of readers to Lorna Byrne – regardless of religious beliefs – is that she gives them back hope, helping them to realise that no matter how alone they might feel they have a guardian angel by their side.

Lorna Byrne sees and talks with angels every day and has done since she was a baby. She sees them as clearly as the rest of us see rocks and stones and trees. In *Stairways to Heaven* Lorna tells true-life stories about the ways that angels help us. She describes how they helped her pull her own life together after her husband died and how she has seen them help other people.

Stairways to Heaven includes never before revealed secrets of your guardian angel, including how your guardian angel was chosen, how you are the only person this angel will ever come to earth with, and how you know your guardian angel's name . . . even if you have forgotten it.

'Gives hope and a sense of peace, something that the Church, in many instances, has been unable to do.'

The Times

CORONET

10% of the author's royalties from the sale of *Stairways to Heaven* are being donated to charity. For details of the charities benefiting please see www.lornabyrne.com

ALSO BY LORNA BYRNE

Angels in my Hair

Angels in my Hair is the autobiography of a modern-day mystic, an Irish woman with powers of the saints of old.

When she was a child, people thought Lorna was 'retarded' because she did not seem to be focusing on the world around her. Instead, Lorna was seeing angels and spirits.

As Lorna tells the story of her life, the reader meets, as she did, the creatures from the spirit worlds who also inhabit our own – mostly angels of an astonishing beauty and variety – including the prophet Elijah and an Archangel – but also the spirits of people who have died.

This remarkable book is the testimony of a woman who sees things beyond the range of our everyday experience.

'Those who see angels are close to being angels. In this book, Lorna beautifully and graphically describes angels and how they work.'
William Roache, MBE, author of *Soul on the Street*

'The world has discovered a modest mystic that it might do well to listen to.' *Daily Mail*

'*Angels in my Hair* is a very simply and softly written narrative, one that managed to grip me emotionally (tears were shed) and made me reflect.' *Sunday Independent*

arrow books